PUFI

# SCIENCE IS LIT

PUFFIN BOOKS

UK | USA | Canada | Ireland | Australia
India | New Zealand | South Africa

Penguin Books is part of the Penguin Random House group of companies
whose addresses can be found at global.penguinrandomhouse.com.

www.penguin.co.uk
www.puffin.co.uk
www.ladybird.co.uk

Penguin
Random House
UK

First published 2024
001

Text copyright © Emanuel Wallace, 2024
Illustration copyright © Subi Bosa, 2024

The moral right of the author and illustrator has been asserted

Text Design by Dynamo
Printed and bound in Great Britain by Clays Ltd, Elcograf S.p.A.

The authorized representative in the EEA is Penguin Random House Ireland,
Morrison Chambers, 32 Nassau Street, Dublin D02 YH68

A CIP catalogue record for this book is available from the British Library

ISBN: 978–0–241–65372–2

All correspondence to:
Puffin Books
Penguin Random House Children's
One Embassy Gardens, 8 Viaduct Gardens, London SW11 7BW

Third party web sites or social media platforms may be referred to or
included for information purposes only and the author and publisher accept no
responsibility for, and do not control, approve or endorse any information or
material contained on such third party web sites or social media platforms.

MIX
Paper | Supporting
responsible forestry
FSC
www.fsc.org
FSC® C018179

Penguin Random House is committed to a
sustainable future for our business, our readers
and our planet. This book is made from Forest
Stewardship Council® certified paper.

# TIKTOK SCIENCE SENSATION
# BIG MANNY

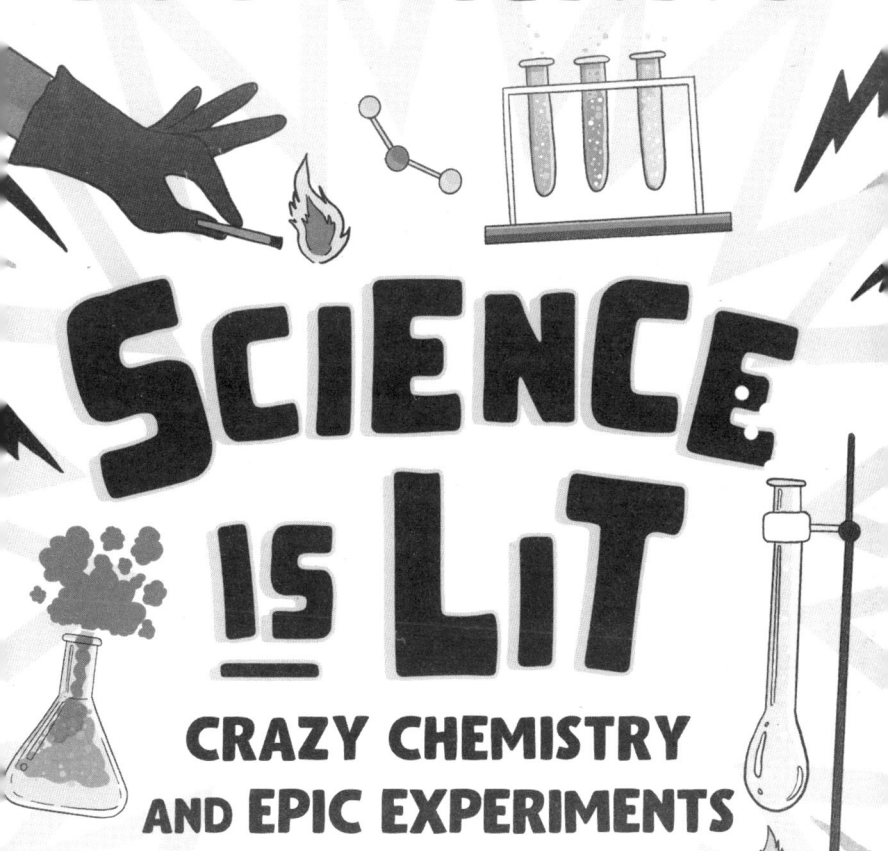

# SCIENCE IS LIT

## CRAZY CHEMISTRY AND EPIC EXPERIMENTS

*ILLUSTRATED BY SUBI BOSA*

PUFFIN

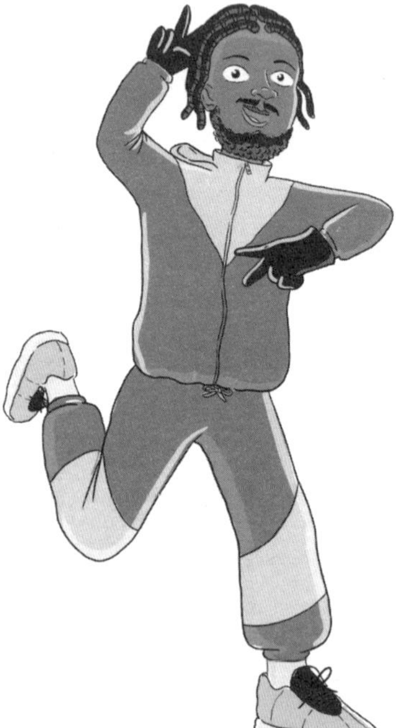

# CONTENTS

**INTRODUCTION** — **01**

**CHAPTER 1: EXPERIMENT TIME** — **13**
★ *EXPERIMENT 1: CAN YOU CYCLE ON SAND?* — 20
   **DIFFICULTY LEVEL:** Simple Ting ⚡

★ *EXPERIMENT 2: TESTING DIFFERENT SURFACES* — 37
   **DIFFICULTY LEVEL:** Simple Ting ⚡

**CHAPTER 2: DO ME A SOLID** — **40**
★ *EXPERIMENT 3: AS COLD AS ICE* — 53
   **DIFFICULTY LEVEL:** Come On Now ⚡⚡🔥

★ *EXPERIMENT 4: SOLID OR LIQUID?* — 55
   **DIFFICULTY LEVEL:** Simple Ting ⚡❄

**CHAPTER 3: MIX IT UP** — **59**
★ *EXPERIMENT 5: CRYSTALLIZATION* — 67
   **DIFFICULTY LEVEL:** Come On Now ⚡⚡🔥

★ *EXPERIMENT 6: SEPARATING SOLIDS* — 74
   **DIFFICULTY LEVEL:** Simple Ting ⚡

★ **EXPERIMENT 7: FILTRATION STATION**    78
  **DIFFICULTY LEVEL:** Come On Now ⚡⚡❄

## CHAPTER 4: LETS SPLIT    **83**
★ **EXPERIMENT 8: CHROMATOGRAPHY**    86
  **DIFFICULTY LEVEL:** Come On Now ⚡⚡

★ **EXPERIMENT 9: DISTILLATION**    91
  **DIFFICULTY LEVEL:** Come On Now ⚡⚡🔥

## CHAPTER 5: COME ON COMBUSTION    **101**
★ **EXPERIMENT 10: OXYGEN IS KEY**    108
  **DIFFICULTY LEVEL:** Come On Now ⚡⚡🔥

★ **EXPERIMENT 11: MAKING SOOT**    121
  **DIFFICULTY LEVEL:** Come On Now ⚡⚡🔥

## CHAPTER 6: I CAN'T ALKALIE    **126**
★ **EXPERIMENT 12: MAKING A RED-CABBAGE INDICATOR**    131
  **DIFFICULTY LEVEL:** Big Science ⚡⚡⚡❄

★ **EXPERIMENT 13: NEUTRALIZATION**    138
  **DIFFICULTY LEVEL:** Big Science ⚡⚡⚡❄

★ **EXPERIMENT 14: MAKING A LAVA LAMP**    145
  **DIFFICULTY LEVEL:** Come On Now ⚡⚡❄

## CHAPTER 7: BOOM — 149
★ EXPERIMENT 154: CORNFLOUR + WATER — 151
   **DIFFICULTY LEVEL:** Simple Ting

★ EXPERIMENT 165: VINEGAR + BAKING SODA — 154
   **DIFFICULTY LEVEL:** Big Science

★ EXPERIMENT 176: INFLATING A BALLOON — 157
   **DIFFICULTY LEVEL:** Big Science

★ EXPERIMENT 18: TURNING MILK INTO PLASTIC — 160
   **DIFFICULTY LEVEL:** Big Science

★ EXPERIMENT 19: ELEPHANT'S TOOTHPASTE — 164
   **DIFFICULTY LEVEL:** Big Science

## CHAPTER 8: EVEN BIGGER SCIENCE — 169
★ EXPERIMENT 20: EXTRACTING DNA — 179
   **DIFFICULTY LEVEL:** Big Science

## SCIENCE LESSON COMPLETED — 183
★ WHICH ELEMENT ARE YOU? — 187

★ BIG MANNY'S BIG QUIZ — 189

★ ANSWERS — 196

★ GLOSSARY — 203

# Hi, I'M EMANUEL – BUT YOU MIGHT KNOW ME AS BIG MANNY.

I'm a scientist who does mad-cool experiments on TikTok. I've even been on TV and done experiments for live audiences. And in this book, I'm going to teach you how to do your own experiments at home and become a real-life scientist, **iNiT**.

Science was always my favourite lesson at school – I used to love all of the big explosions and fiery experiments. I found science fascinating because it taught me about things that I couldn't even see, and that blew my mind!

# INTRODUCTION

Like all of the **microscopic cells** inside of our bodies that keep us alive. They're so tiny, yet so important.

Or the invisible waves that we use every day, like the ones that control our TVs. **How does the remote control the TV without even being connected to it?** Crazy.

**Or what about when you blow on a candle, and it goes out?**

I found myself asking all of these types of questions, and science was the only thing that could provide me with answers. I was so fascinated that I decided to study science at university and ended up with two degrees in biomedical science.

WHAT IS IT ABOUT OUR BREATH THAT MAKES THE CANDLE DO THAT?

# INTRODUCTION

After I graduated, I worked in a school as a science technician, which was my dream! I got to prepare all of the science experiments for the students and show them what to do in class. And now I'm about to share some of this knowledge with you guys at home.

> JUST A QUICK HEADS-UP BEFORE WE GET STARTED: IN THIS BOOK, YOU MIGHT HEAR ME SAY WAGWAN A LOT – IN CASE YOU DON'T KNOW, THAT MEANS WHAT'S GOING ON? SOME OTHER THINGS YOU MIGHT CATCH ME SAYING ARE ITE (ALRIGHT), LIKKLE (LITTLE) AND TING (YOU GUESSED IT, THAT JUST MEANS THING!). OK, NOW LET'S GET INTO IT . . .

INTRODUCTION

# **THINKING LIKE A SCIENTIST**

My journey with science began with me asking lots of questions. In this book, I'm gonna encourage you to ask some of your own and start *thinking like a scientist*. Like:

### **WHY DO LEMONS TASTE SOUR?**

### **WHY DO METALS FEEL COLD WHEN YOU TOUCH THEM?**

### **WHY ARE FLAMES YELLOW?**

Every scientific discovery starts with a question. And they don't have to be big, complicated questions either. Science is used in literally everything we do, and we don't even realize. It can be as simple as:

- ★ **Making a cuppa.** When we add hot water to a teabag, the tea **diffuses** (or spreads out) from the teabag and into the water, making it change colour.

- ★ **Baking a cake.** One of the ingredients in a cake mixture is baking soda – otherwise

# INTRODUCTION

known as **sodium bicarbonate**. This ingredient releases loads of gas when we heat it in the oven. This gas release causes the cake to rise and become nice and fluffy. If we didn't have sodium bicarbonate in cakes then they would stay flat.

★ **Eating food.** When you swallow food, it goes into a sea of **hydrochloric acid** in your stomach (we'll find out more about acids later!). The hydrochloric acid breaks down the food into smaller pieces so that it's easier for you to digest.

Science is way more than just a lesson you do at school. Science is all around us – in how we cook, eat, heat our homes, power our cars and *loads* more stuff that won't fit on this page.

You've probably heard of chemistry, but you might not start studying it until you get to secondary school. Man's gonna teach you some basic chemistry tings now that are gonna be useful as you read this book and will help you understand the cool experiments we're gonna try!

INTRODUCTION

## CHEMISTRY TING

Chemistry is the study of **matter**, which is basically all the stuff in the universe. Matter comes in three different forms: **solids**, **liquids** and **gases**. You are made of matter, and so is this book.

Chemistry looks at the behaviour, structure and properties of matter. This sounds complicated but really what we're talking about are things like how hard or soft something is, how it moves or what happens when you put it in water.

**Like, will a piece of wood float or sink? Or what happens when I pour sand into a bucket?**

SiMPLE TiNGS.

## ELEMENTS, ATOMS AND MOLECULES

When we break matter down into its simplest form, what we're left with is an **element**. An element is a substance that can't be broken down into smaller parts or changed into something else.

Elements are made of **atoms**, which are like tiny building blocks that make up everything in the universe. Like how Lego bricks are used to build a

## INTRODUCTION

Lego house. Elements consist of only one type of atom – so imagine a Lego house with all the same-coloured bricks.

A **molecule** is two or more atoms that are bonded together. A chemical bond is an attraction between atoms that holds them together. Molecules can be made of the same type of atom, or different atoms – like two different-coloured pieces of Lego stuck together. One example of a molecule is water, which is two hydrogen atoms bonded with one oxygen atom, or $H_2O$. The number 2 after the H tells us that there are two hydrogen atoms, and the single O tells us that there is one oxygen atom.

A **particle** is a **microscopic** (so small we can't see it without a microscope) piece of matter, and it can mean both atoms and molecules. For example, we can call a water molecule a water particle.

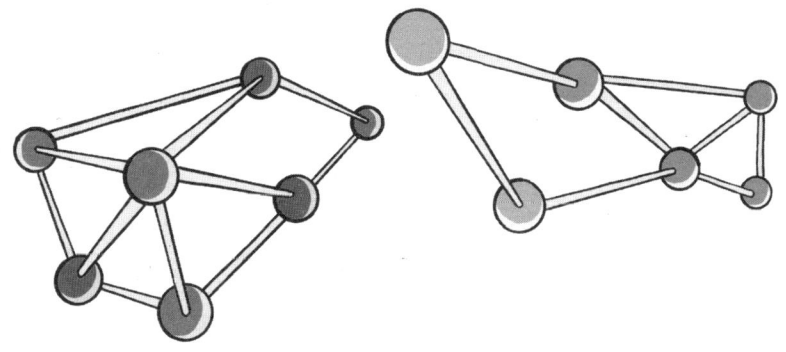

## INTRODUCTION

## THE ELEMENTS IN THE ROOM

OK, now man knows what an element is, I'm gonna introduce you to some key elements you'll find in this book. You can think of them like a bunch of characters with different personalities. And experiments can teach us how these different characters are gonna react to each other.

One of the key elements that we're gonna meet is the main man **OXYGEN**. Oxygen is everywhere – you can't escape it. You're literally breathing some in right now! Oxygen really loves to get lit, and I mean that literally. Oxygen is the key ingredient needed for a fire to start. If there's a fire going down, then you can guarantee that oxygen will be the life of the party.

Next up we have hydrogen. Now **HYDROGEN** is very close with oxygen. They're like a super-tight couple. Hydrogen is kind of **similar** to oxygen because it loves to get lit too! Maybe even a bit too lit at times. When hydrogen and oxygen bond together, they cool each other right down and form water ($H_2O$).

We're also going to meet **CARBON**, another friend of oxygen. Carbon is full of energy but can be a bit of a hothead sometimes. It's one of the main elements inside fuels like charcoal and petrol. Carbon loves being burned! After a heated session, carbon likes to chill with oxygen. The two bond to form **CARBON DIOXIDE**. That's the gas that we breathe out.

## INTRODUCTION

**SODIUM** is another element that pops up quite a bit, and sodium is a real bad man, trust me! You don't want to mess with sodium. But actually it can be a real softie sometimes too.

Lastly we have an element called **CHLORINE**. Now chlorine loves to spend lots of time with sodium – they're like another close couple. Sodium and chlorine do split up from time to time, but they always come back together.

Some of the elements are really hyped up and excited and they love to react with other elements.

# INTRODUCTION

What do I mean by react? Well, when different elements react with each other, they form new bonds and create new substances. For example, sodium reacts with chlorine to form sodium chloride, otherwise known as table salt.

Not all elements like to react with other elements though. Some of them are happy just chilling by themselves, so they're less reactive – meaning, less likely to react with other elements.

OK, now that we've got the basics down, it's time to start experimenting. Throughout this book, you'll see I've rated the experiments as either **SIMPLE TING** (easy), **COME ON NOW** (medium) or **BIG SCIENCE** (advanced). The **SIMPLE TING** experiments are designed to be easy enough that you can do them by yourself. If I say **COME ON NOW**, you may need an adult to help you, so ask an adult to be present. And when you get to **BIG SCIENCE**, this is proper advanced science so defo ask an adult and don't try these alone! To help you out, some of the experiments include example results from me, and other times I've left you to add your own results.

11

## INTRODUCTION

You'll also spot a couple of safety symbols that appear on the tougher experiments where you'll need an adult.

This flame symbol means we'll be using heat . . .

. . . and the splat symbol means the experiment could get messy!

As well as awesome experiments, this book is packed with scientific knowledge – some of this is simple stuff, but some of it is bare challenging to **LEVEL UP** your science game. Have a go at the tougher stuff where you see the arrow symbol, or if you want to skip it and just try the experiment, that's cool too fam.

If you don't know what all the words mean, there's also a glossary starting on p.203 to help you.

Let's get started and find out what we need to create our own experiments.

# CHAPTER 1
# EXPERIMENT TIME

## CHAPTER 1

**BOOM!** The first thing that we need to be a scientist is a **hypothesis**. That sounds like a mad word but it's an easy ting, trust me. A hypothesis is basically what we think is going to happen in the experiment. So let's say the experiment is putting two different types of tea bag into cold water and seeing what colour the water turns. Our hypothesis could be that we think tea bag number one will turn the water a darker brown than tea bag number two.

The next ting that we need is a **method**. A method is just the steps to do the experiment. So let's take the tea bag experiment again.

**The method for this experiment is:**

- ★ Put 200ml cold water into two cups.
- ★ Place each tea bag into a cup of water.
- ★ See what colour the water turns.

The method also comes with an equipment list. An equipment list is the list of everything needed to do the experiment.

### EXPERIMENT TIME

So for this experiment, that would include:

- ★ Two clear glasses or cups
- ★ 200ml cold water
- ★ Two types of tea bag

> **ITE, SO WAGWAN FOR THE RESULTS NOW?**

The results are what happened in the experiment. So in this experiment, your results would show what colour the water turned when you added the two different tea bags. Simple ting.

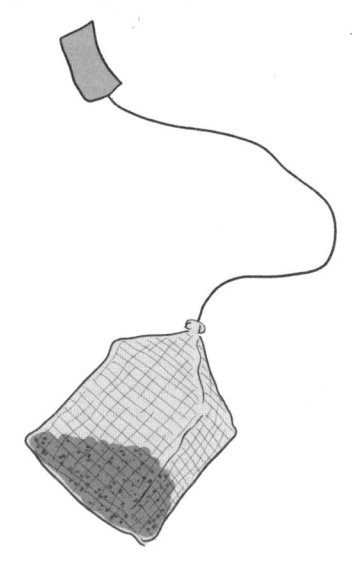

## CHAPTER 1

The last thing that we need to become a real-life scientist is a conclusion. Again, I know that word sounds like a mad ting but it's not even that mad, trust me. Man's gonna tell you what a conclusion is now. Remember our hypothesis at the beginning, when we said that tea bag number one will turn the water a darker brown than tea bag number two? The conclusion is just whether our hypothesis was correct or not.

> SO DID TEA BAG ONE TURN THE WATER A DARKER BROWN?

> YES, IT DID.

**So, were we correct?** Yes, we were.

So in our conclusion we say that our hypothesis was correct and the result of the experiment was what we expected.

# EXPERIMENT TIME

## CONTROLS

If you want to be a scientist, it's very important that you know what **controls** are. Controls are the things in the experiment that scientists keep the same. Let's look at the teabag example again. It is important that we pour the same amount of water into each cup, so that we don't accidentally change our results because one cup had more water in it than the other. It's also really important that we keep the temperature of the water the same both times, because this could also affect how the water changes colour. The controls in this experiment are making sure that we use the same amount of water at the same temperature for each cup, so that we can get the correct results.

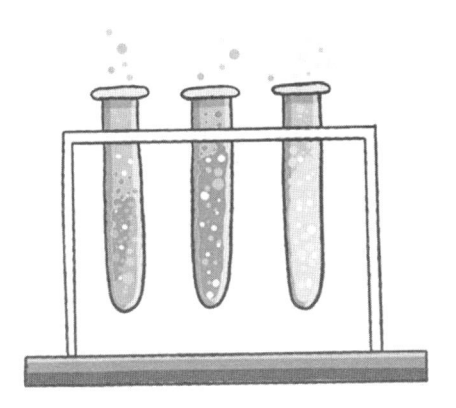

## HOW TO BE SAFE

Ite cool, safety is bare important still, I can't lie. Before we do any experiments, here are some important steps to follow:

★ Scientists always wear goggles when we're doing experiments to protect our eyes. Goggles make sure that no liquids splash into our eyes and hurt us.

> ! If you don't have lab goggles at home, swimming goggles also work fine for home experiments!

★ Whenever we are doing an experiment, we should always be standing up. If something spills, it's easier to move out of the way if we are standing up instead of sitting down. (If you are a wheelchair user or if standing for periods of time might be hard for you, have a chat to your grown-up to work out the best way to conduct the experiment safely together.)

★ If you have any pets or younger brothers or sisters, make sure they're safely out of the way!

- ★ Make sure to dispose of any mixtures safely. If you're not sure of the best way to do this, ask a grown-up for their advice. And remember to clear up any mess afterwards (we don't want to be slipping and sliding around!).

- ★ When using liquids, put down some newspaper or old tea towels on your work surface and floor – in case things get messy. And always wash your hands after experiments.

- ★ If anything does splash into your eyes or on to your skin, wash with plenty of cold water.

- ★ Another safety rule is not eating or drinking when we are doing an experiment. This is to make sure that the chemicals that we are using don't get into our food. We wouldn't want to accidentally eat some of the experiment! That would be a mad ting.

- ★ Lastly, we never run around while doing an experiment as we wouldn't want to knock any chemicals over.

**DIFFICULTY LEVEL:**
　Simple Ting ⚡

# EXPERIMENT 1:
# CAN YOU CYCLE ON SAND?

BOOM! Let's think of our next big question now and try our first proper experiment. Which surface is the easiest to cycle on: concrete, grass or sand? Now the test that we're going to use is called a comparative test, cos we're going to be *comparing* the different surfaces, init. A comparative test is where you test or compare different materials or objects and look at how they might behave differently.

We're going to ride the bike on the concrete, grass and sand, and test the difficulty of each one. Simple tings. If you don't live near somewhere where there's sand, you

> **ROADS CAN BE DANGEROUS, FAM, SO NEVER CYCLE ON A BUSY ROAD OR NEAR TRAFFIC!**

could try cycling on gravel or a muddy path instead. Next ting we need is a hypothesis, or prediction. Now I think that the concrete is going to be the easiest, to be honest, followed by the grass and then the sand. The sand will defo be the most difficult. Cool, so that's our hypothesis, done know. The next ting we need is some equipment and that.

So this is our equipment list:

- ★ a helmet
- ★ a bike
- ★ different surfaces to cycle on (concrete, grass and sand)
- ★ a piece of paper
- ★ a pen

Now we need our method. How exactly are we going to do this experiment? We're going to put on a helmet and get a bike, then cycle for fifteen seconds on the concrete. After fifteen seconds, we'll stop the bike and rate how difficult it was to ride. Then we do the same thing on sand and grass.

**WAIT, HOLD UP...**

**What exactly are we going to be measuring in this experiment?** We're going to be measuring how difficult it is to cycle on each surface. The way we will measure this is by rating the difficulty on a scale from 1–10. 1 means that it's bare easy and 10 means it's difficult. The thing that you measure during an experiment is called the **dependent variable**.

In this experiment, the dependent variable is how hard it is to cycle.

**What are we going to be changing in this experiment?**
The type of surface we cycle on — concrete, grass and sand. The thing that you change during an experiment is called the **independent variable**.

So in this experiment, the independent variable is the type of surface, because that's what we're changing, init. You done know, come on.

**Remember we spoke about the controls earlier on?**

So, in this experiment the control (the thing we're going to keep the same) is the bike.

OBVIOUSLY WE CAN'T USE DIFFERENT BIKES AND THAT COS SOME BIKES MIGHT BE FASTER THAN OTHERS SO THAT WOULD MAKE THE RESULTS **INVALID**, INIT.

We'll use the same bike to make sure that the experiment is being done fairly and the results are 100% certified. Come on. So our control is using the same bike for each surface.

Now we have everything we need to begin our scientific write-up — where we write down the purpose of our experiment, our hypothesis, results and conclusion.

# SCIENTIFIC WRITE-UP

## AIM OF INVESTIGATION (What are you trying to find out?):
Which surface is easiest to cycle on: concrete, grass or sand?

## HYPOTHESIS (What do you predict will happen?):
I predict that the concrete will be the easiest to cycle on, followed by grass and then sand.

## EQUIPMENT: helmet, bike, concrete, grass, sand, pen, paper

## METHOD:
1. Put on helmet.
2. Ride bike for fifteen seconds on the concrete.
3. Write down how difficult it was on a scale of 1–10.
4. Repeat for grass and sand.

## VARIABLE I WILL CHANGE (independent variable):
Type of surface (grass, sand, concrete)

## VARIABLE I WILL MEASURE (dependent variable):
Difficulty of cycling

## THINGS I WILL KEEP THE SAME (controls):
Type of bike

# RESULTS

| SURFACE TYPE | DIFFICULTY RATING (1–10) |
|---|---|
| Concrete | 2 |
| Grass | 4 |
| Sand | 10 |

The results from a comparative test would be used to make a bar chart like this. We can see that this chart compares more than one independent variable — these are the categories listed along the bottom of the chart.

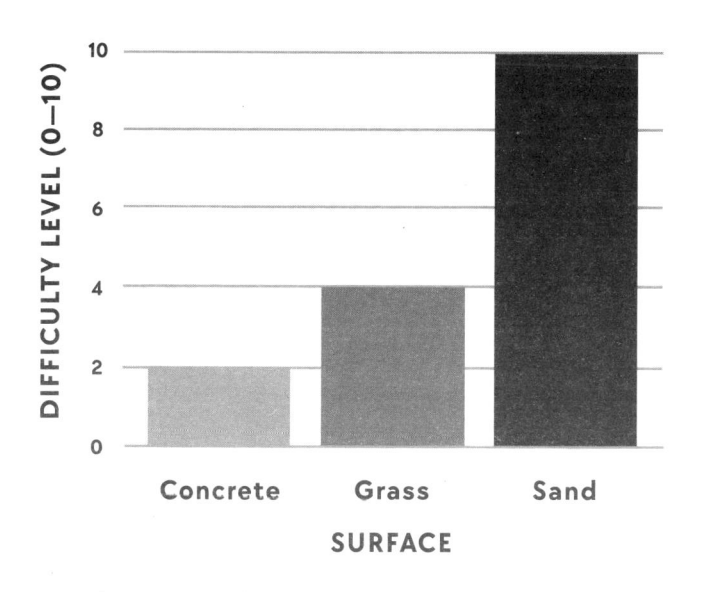

The numbers going up on the left-hand side of the chart are the difficulty levels of each variable.

If you look at sand, for example, the bar for sand reaches number ten on our difficulty-level scale — so we know that sand is rated ten.

## CONCLUSION

Ite cool, we need a conclusion ting. Remember, all you need to do for the conclusion is say whether the prediction that you made in your hypothesis was correct or not. We predicted that the concrete would be the easiest to cycle on, followed by the grass and then sand. If we take a look at our results, we can see that the concrete was the easiest because it had the lowest difficulty rating of two. The sand was the most difficult because it had the highest rating of ten, and grass was in the middle at four. So our prediction was correct! Our conclusion is that the concrete is the easiest surface to cycle on, followed by grass and then sand.

BOOM! DONE KNOW! BIG TINGS.

# EXPERIMENT TIME

## EVALUATION

As proper scientists, we want to make sure our experiments are bang on in terms of their **accuracy** and **precision**. Let's break down what we mean by accuracy and precise.

**Accuracy** is when our results are close to the correct result.

**Precision** is when we repeat the experiment more than once and get similar results each time.

To be more accurate, you can make sure you're using the right tools to measure your results – for example, using a beaker with measurements on the side will be more accurate than using a regular glass.

*YOU DONE KNOW!*

It's actually easy to be more precise. You just have to repeat the experiment more than once and make sure your results are similar each time you repeat the experiment.

Take a look at the pictures on the next page to see the difference between accuracy and precision.

## CHAPTER 1

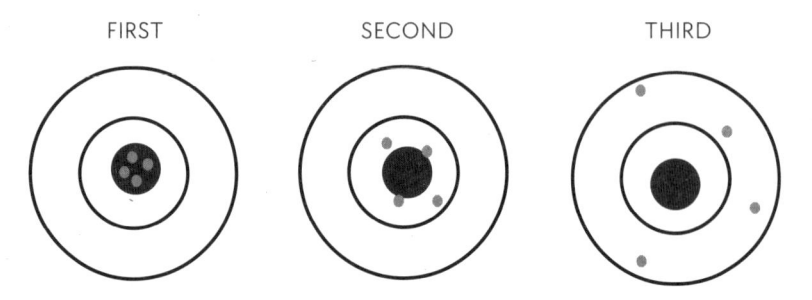

FIRST　　　　　　　SECOND　　　　　　THIRD

## ACCURACY

On these dart boards, the dark circle in the middle represents the correct result that we are trying to reach, and the grey dots represent the results of our experiments. If the grey dots are inside or close to the dark centre of the board, then the results are accurate. If the dots are outside the dark centre, then they're inaccurate.

We can see on the first dart board that the results are right in the middle, so they're very accurate. On the second dart board, the grey dots aren't quite inside the centre but they're really close, so they're still pretty accurate. On the third dart board, the dots are really far from the centre, so they're inaccurate. Come on!

## EXPERIMENT TIME

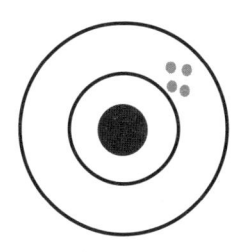

## PRECISION

On this board, all of the grey dots are outside of the centre, so they're inaccurate. But they *are* precise! All of the dots are close together, so the results are all similar. This makes them precise.

Your **evaluation** is when you look at how the experiment can be improved to make it more accurate and/or precise. So how could we have made our cycling experiment more accurate? Well, we could have used a stopwatch to time the fifteen seconds instead of counting them. A stopwatch would've allowed us to measure time more accurately. And to make the experiment more precise, we just need to repeat the experiment a few times and make sure we get similar results. BOOM! That's your evaluation done.

## CHAPTER 1

# WHAT'S A FAIR TEST?

Ite cool, the two main types of tests are fair tests and comparative tests. You've heard about a comparative test already, but how is it different from a fair test?

In a fair test, you only change one variable, init. For example, in the teabag experiment we only changed the type of teabag and everything else was kept the same – including the amount of water and the temperature. We have more control over the variables in fair tests and they're usually carried out in a **controlled environment**, such as a science lab. You get me?

*LET'S TAKE A LiKKLE LOOK . . .*

In a comparative test, we have less control over the variables. Let's look at the cycling experiment again. In this test there are many variables that are out of our control.

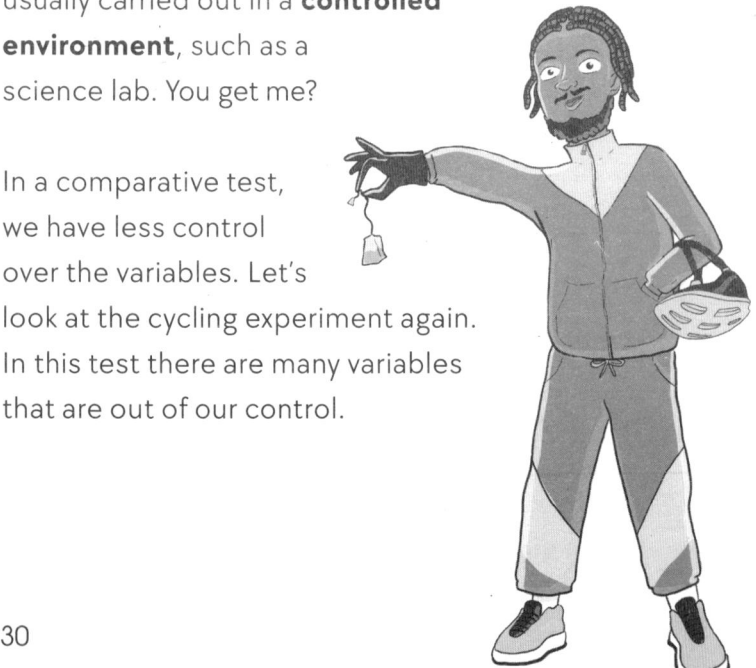

## EXPERIMENT TIME

> THE CONCRETE MIGHT HAVE CRACKS IN IT WHICH MAKE IT HARDER TO CYCLE, OR MAYBE IT STARTS TO RAIN AND THE GRASS GETS EXTRA SLIPPERY! CYCLING WOULD BE A MAD TING IN THOSE CONDITIONS.

It's impossible to keep everything exactly the same in a comparative test, but we can still use controls to make our results more accurate – like using the same bike each time.

**Can you work out which of the tests below are fair tests, and which ones are comparative tests? I've given you an example to start you off! To find the answers, flick to p.198.**

1. **Rolling a tennis ball down ramps of different heights and seeing how far it travels.** This is a fair test, because we are only changing one variable – the height of the ramp.

2. **Driving two toy cars down a ramp and seeing how far each one travels.**

31

## CHAPTER 1

3. **Removing oxygen from a lit candle (we'll try this experiment later in the book!).**

4. **Seeing which tissue soaks up more water.**

5. **Seeing which material is most reflective.**

Ite cool, now we're going to take a look at a fair test. This experiment involves adding different weights to an elastic band to see how far it stretches. We can hypothesize that the more weight that is added to the elastic band, the further it will stretch. So the results for this fair test would look something like this:

| WEIGHT ADDED TO ELASTIC | LENGTH OF ELASTIC BAND |
|---|---|
| 0g | 5cm |
| 10g | 8cm |
| 20g | 12cm |
| 30g | 18cm |

# EXPERIMENT TIME

The **data** from this fair test – that's the information we recorded in the experiment – can be put into a graph like this. Unlike the bar chart, the line graph only measures one type of independent variable, which is why we use it in fair tests.

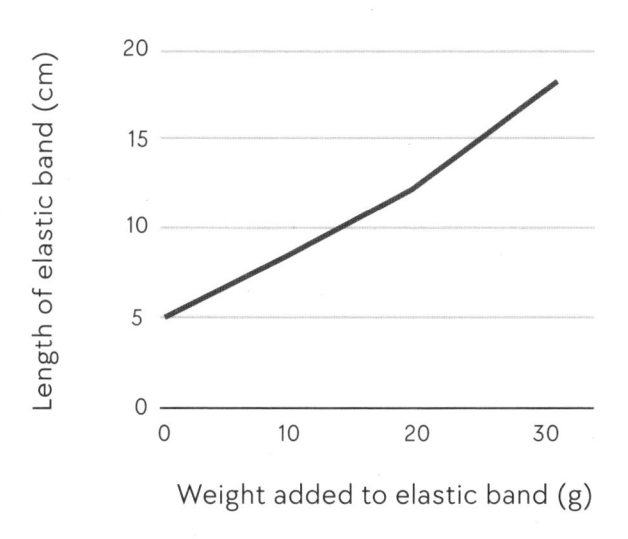

Weight added to elastic band (g)

## SPOT THE PATTERN

Let's do a likkle analysis on these results and see wagwan. **Can we see any patterns or trends in the data?**

**First of all, what's the independent variable (thing we are changing) in this experiment?**
The weight added to the elastic band.

## CHAPTER 1

**What's the dependent variable (thing we are measuring)?**
The length of the elastic band.

The numbers along the bottom of the graph are the different weights. The numbers going up the left-hand side are the different lengths that the rubber band stretched to. Put your finger at the start of the black line and follow it to the end. As you go past 10g, 20g and 30g, the line goes higher up the graph. This means that the length of the elastic band is increasing as more weight is added.

So we can clearly see that as we increase the *weight* added to the elastic band, the *length* of the elastic band also increases. This means that there is a **correlation** between the two variables. Correlation sounds like a mad word but it just means that there's a relationship between the two variables. So as the independent variable (the weight) increases, so does the dependent variable (the length). **Easy ting**.

EXPERIMENT TIME

## A DIFFERENT FAIR TEST

Let's go back to the first fair-test example from those questions I gave you. I build three ramps of different heights from the same material. One ramp is 50cm high, the next one is 30cm high and the last one 10cm high. Then I let a tennis ball roll down from the top of each ramp one by one and measure the distance the tennis ball travels.
Our results would look something similar to this:

| RAMP HEIGHT | DISTANCE BALL TRAVELLED |
|---|---|
| 10cm | 2m |
| 30cm | 6m |
| 50cm | 10m |

These results can be used to make a line graph like the one on the next page.

# CHAPTER 1

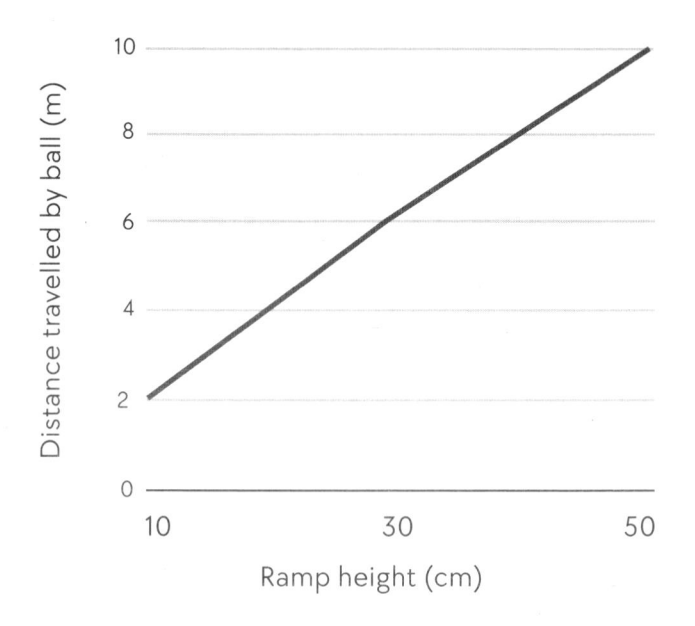

*[Graph: Distance travelled by ball (m) vs Ramp height (cm), showing a straight line increasing from about 2 m at 10 cm to 10 m at 50 cm]*

Once again, we can see a correlation between these two variables. As we increase the height of the ramp (the independent variable), the distance the ball travels (the dependent variable) also increases. This means that the height of the ramp is **directly proportional** to the distance the ball travels. Directly proportional is just a fancy way of saying that they both increase at the same rate.

COME ON, FAM

**DIFFICULTY LEVEL:** Simple Ting ⚡

# EXPERIMENT 2:
# TESTING DIFFERENT SURFACES

**ITE, BOOM!** For our second experiment I'm gonna give you a scientific write-up and you're gonna fill in the blanks, yeah? Cool, let's go. If you need some help, take a look at p.199.

**EXPERIMENT AIM:** Does a toy car travel further on a wooden floor or a carpet?

## HYPOTHESIS:

_____

_____

_____

## EQUIPMENT:

This is our equipment list:
- ★ a toy car
- ★ wooden or laminate floor
- ★ a tape measure
- ★ carpet

## METHOD:

1. Push toy car on wooden/laminate floor and measure distance travelled.

2. Repeat for carpet and measure distance travelled. Make sure you push the car just as hard on the carpet as you did on the wooden/laminate floor, but not harder.

**VARIABLE I WILL CHANGE** (independent variable):

**VARIABLE I WILL MEASURE** (dependent variable):

**THINGS I WILL KEEP THE SAME** (control):

## RESULTS

| FLOOR TYPE | DISTANCE TRAVELLED BY CAR (CM) |
|---|---|
| Wood/laminate | |
| Carpet | |

## CONCLUSION

(Was your prediction correct? And do you think this is a fair test or a comparative one?)

**Now you know how to do experiments safely and fairly – nice one!**

ITE COOL

Let's remind ourselves of everything we just learned in this chapter:

★ A hypothesis or prediction is what you think will happen.

★ We use controls to make our results accurate and valid (that just means how true the results are).

★ The data from a fair test can be used to make a line graph.

★ The data from a comparative test can be used to make a bar chart.

★ The dependent variable is the thing we are measuring.

★ The independent variable is the thing that we change.

# CHAPTER 2

# DO ME A SOLID

## DO ME A SOLID

Ite, **BOOM!** I can't lie – I'm feeling kinda gassed right now, so let's talk about solids, liquids and gases.

Every kind of substance can exist as either a solid, liquid or gas – we call these the three states of matter. Let's take water ($H_2O$) for example.

**What is water when it's a solid?**
Take a look in your freezer or ice box and you'll see it: ice cubes! Ice is just solid water.

**What's liquid water?**
Well, liquid water is obviously the water that we drink, init.

**But what about water when it's a gas?**
Think about what happens when a kettle boils. You see all of that steam coming out of the spout? That's water in the form of a gas. It's called water vapour and it's what clouds are made of! When water turns into water vapour, it's a process called **evaporation**. Water evaporates from the seas and turns into water vapour, and when the water **particles** in the air clump together, they form clouds. You done know, come on.

# CHAPTER 2

# WHAT'S THE DIFFERENCE BETWEEN SOLIDS, LIQUIDS AND GASES?

Wood, paper and metal are all examples of solids. These solids are made up of tiny particles arranged in a particular way to create a solid structure. In a solid, the particles are packed together really tightly, so they can't move around that much.

If we zoomed in on a solid, it would look like this:

**Solid**

## DO ME A SOLID

**So what makes the particles pack together so tightly in solids?**
It's because of the forces of attraction between them. Kind of like they're being pulled together by a really strong magnet. The particles are held in a fixed position but they're also **vibrating** – which means they're sort of shaking but standing in the same place.

Liquids, on the other hand, can move around because the particles aren't packed together so tightly. They're still close together, but there are some gaps. The forces of attraction in liquids are weaker, so the particles can separate from each other. It's like they're holding hands loosely, so they can easily let go.

> THAT'S WHY WE CAN POUR LIQUIDS LIKE ORANGE JUICE AND THAT, YOU GET ME?

## CHAPTER 2

The particles in a liquid are arranged in a random way and look like this:

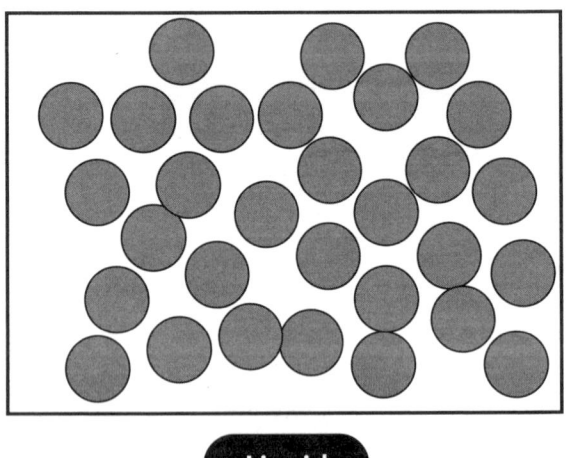

**Liquid**

**Ite cool, so we've looked at the particles in solids and liquids – what about the particles in gases?** Gas particles are spread out bare far away from each other, so there are bigger gaps between them. Similar to liquid particles, gas particles also have weak forces of attraction, so the particles can separate from each other. This means that the gas particles are free to move in any direction and have a random arrangement like liquids. Some examples of gases are **HELiUM**, which we use to make floaty balloons; **CARBON DiOXiDE**, which we breathe out; and **OXYGEN** – which we breathe in!

**DO ME A SOLID**

Gas particles look like this:

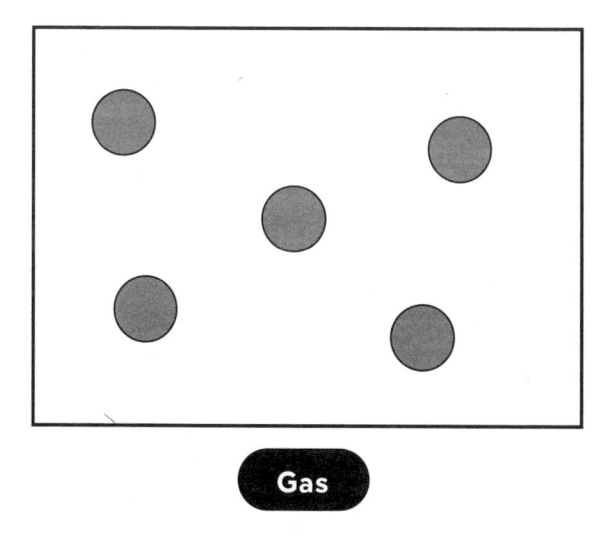

**Gas**

However, unlike liquids, gases are easy to **compress** – basically that means *squashed*. The reason why gases can be compressed is because there are large spaces between the particles, so we can bring the particles in closer together and close these gaps. Solids and liquids, on the other hand, only have small gaps between their particles, so they can't be squashed any closer together. So gases can change their **volume**, or how much space they take up, while solids and liquids can't.

## CHAPTER 2

|        | CAN YOU HOLD IT EASILY? | DOES IT CHANGE ITS SHAPE? | DOES IT CHANGE ITS VOLUME? |
|--------|-------------------------|---------------------------|----------------------------|
| Solid  | YES                     | NO                        | NO                         |
| Liquid | NO                      | YES                       | NO                         |
| Gas    | NO                      | YES                       | YES                        |

Now we're going to do a quick activity. Below we have a list of different solids, liquids and gases. Can you identify which state of matter each substance is? Once you're done, take a look at the answers on p.199 to see if you're right.

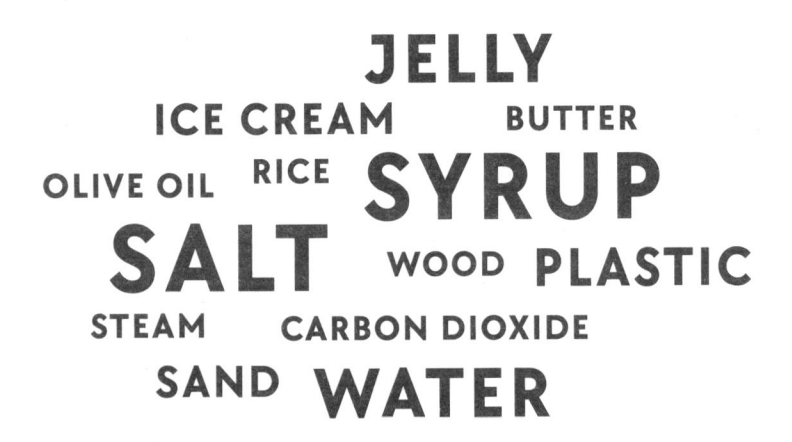

**JELLY**
**ICE CREAM** **BUTTER**
**OLIVE OIL** **RICE** **SYRUP**
**SALT** **WOOD** **PLASTIC**
**STEAM** **CARBON DIOXIDE**
**SAND** **WATER**

## DO ME A SOLID

# MATTER IS A WHOLE MOOD

Another way of thinking about solids, liquids and gases is as different *moods* that matter can switch between.

Let's look at our old friend $H_2O$. $H_2O$ has three moods: sleepy, awake and excited. These different moods represent the three states of matter: solid, liquid and gas.

## SLEEPY

When $H_2O$ is in solid form, it's like they're a bit sleepy – their particles don't have enough energy to move around very much.

Solid water – or ice – keeps its shape, 'cos those particles aren't going anywhere. Solids can be cut and shaped and they always take up the same amount of space.

MAN'S FEELING A BIT SLEEPY, YOU KNOW. I DIDN'T GET MUCH REST LAST NIGHT STILL.

## CHAPTER 2

### AWAKE

When H$_2$O starts waking up, they get more energy and start moving about a bit. Let's say they've arrived at school by now and they're starting to switch on their brain.

*ITE, LET'S SEE WAGWAN WITH THIS TING.*

When a solid is turned into a liquid, it's called **melting**. The solid is heated up and it absorbs energy, causing it to melt into a liquid. The temperature at which a solid melts is called its **melting point**. So H$_2$O gets more energetic as they move from their sleepy (solid) state to their awake (liquid) state.

As a solid gets hotter, it **expands** because the particles are moving around more. The particles get further apart as they are heated and the size of the gaps between them increases.

## DO ME A SOLID

Think about an ice cube that's been left out on the table – it warms up and starts to melt. When that ice has turned into liquid, it flows easily and can be poured. It's difficult to hold a liquid in your hand because, unlike in a solid, the particles move freely.

### EXCITED

When $H_2O$ is really excited, they get LOADS of energy and start bouncing around. Maybe $H_2O$'s on their way home from school and they're gassed about what they're gonna eat later!

MAN IS BARE EXCITED ABOUT THE JERK CHICKEN WITH RICE AND PEAS I'VE GOT FOR DINNER!

# CHAPTER 2

When water goes from a liquid into a gas, it's called **boiling**. When a liquid is heated, it absorbs energy and lots of bubbles are created as it boils into a gas. $H_2O$ is getting really energetic now as they move into their excited (gas) state.

Water boils at a temperature of 100° **Celsius**. But water can also change into a gas at a lower temperature – but more slowly – through evaporation. Think of a puddle drying up on a warm day – it doesn't disappear all at once. Instead, the water particles evaporate slowly to become water vapour.

Gases spread out everywhere and change their shape and volume to fill up the container that they're in. Gases are often invisible and can be compressed.

DO ME A SOLID

## H₂O CHILLS OUT

We've seen H₂O turn from sleepy to awake to excited – but what about the other way round?

When a gas turns into a liquid it's called **condensation**. An example of condensation is when water vapour in the bathroom cools down into a liquid when it touches the cold glass of the mirror.

So as H₂O cools, it loses energy and moves from its excited (gas) state to its awake (liquid) state.

When water turns from a liquid into a solid, it's called **freezing**. Water freezes into solid ice at 0° Celsius. When water is frozen, the molecules gradually get cooler in temperature. As they cool down, the water particles lose energy and move around less. When the water particles are moving around less, they can no longer slide over each other and flow like a liquid. They become fixed into their positions and the water turns into a solid.

H₂O is feeling really chilled out now and they've used up all their energy, so they're back in their sleepy (solid) state.

# CHAPTER 2

> I'M FEELING KINDA TIRED NOW. I THINK IT'S A BEDTIME TING.

Let's quickly test our knowledge on the changing states of matter. Take a look at these changes of state below and write down whether they are freezing, melting, evaporating, boiling or condensing. When you're done, flick to p.199 to check your answers.

**Solid** ⟶ **Liquid** = _____

**Liquid** ⟶ **Solid** = _____

**Gas** ⟶ **Liquid** = _____

**Liquid** ⟶ **Gas** = _____

**DIFFICULTY LEVEL:**
Come On Now

# EXPERIMENT 3: AS COLD AS ICE

> Ask a grown-up to help you with this one!

> LET'S LOOK AT A LiKKLE EXPERiMENT TO DO WiTH SOLiDS, LiQUiDS AND GASES.

What we're gonna do, yeah, is find out what happens when you heat up ice and water.

The first thing we need is a hypothesis. So I think that when you heat up the ice, it will melt into a liquid. I also think that when you heat up the liquid, it will boil into a gas. That's our hypothesis, yeah. Cool.

This is our equipment list:
- ★ a pair of goggles
- ★ some ice
- ★ a saucepan
- ★ a hob

## METHOD

1. Put your goggles on.
2. Put some ice cubes into the saucepan.
3. Turn on the hob and heat up the saucepan.
4. Look at what happens to the ice as it is heated up.
5. Look at what happens to the water as it's heated up too.

## RESULTS

We saw that as the ice was heated up in the saucepan, it melted into a liquid. As the liquid was heated further, it began to boil and release bubbles. The water was then boiled into a gas. OK cool, let's make a conclusion now.

## CONCLUSION

Did we make the right prediction? We did! We said that the ice would melt into a liquid and that's what happened. The water also boiled into a gas, so we were correct!

**DIFFICULTY LEVEL:**
Simple Ting

# EXPERIMENT 4: SOLID OR LIQUID?

Ite, BOOM! Here's our next experiment. Let's get some different solids and liquids, and compare their properties.

**What kind of test do you think this is?**

> IF YOU SAID A COMPARATIVE TEST – WOAH! MAN'S A BIG SCIENTIST ALREADY!

OK, for our equipment list we'll need:
- ★ 5 cups
- ★ some water
- ★ a bowl
- ★ runny honey (3 tablespoons)
- ★ sand (3 tablespoons) (sugar granules or crumbled-up biscuits will also work)
- ★ cooking oil (3 tablespoons)
- ★ dough (50g) (you could use pre-made pastry dough, or play-doh!)
- ★ rice (or dried pasta) (half a cup)

> **IF YOU DON'T HAVE ANY HONEY, MIX TWO TABLESPOONS OF SUGAR WITH ONE TABLESPOON OF WATER TO CREATE A SIMILAR SUBSTANCE**

## METHOD

1. One at a time, try to pour each of the materials from the cup into the bowl. **Can you do it?**

2. Next, we're going to touch each of these materials. **Which ones make your hand feel wet?**

> THIS CAN GET MESSY, FAM, SO MAKE SURE YOU'RE STANDING NEAR THE SINK SO YOU CAN WASH YOUR HANDS AFTERWARDS!

Record your findings in this table below.

|  | CAN YOU POUR IT? | DOES IT FEEL WET? | SOLID OR LIQUID? |
|---|---|---|---|
| WATER |  |  |  |
| HONEY |  |  |  |
| SAND |  |  |  |
| OIL |  |  |  |
| DOUGH |  |  |  |
| RICE/ PASTA |  |  |  |

## CONCLUSION

BOOM! So we can conclude that water, runny honey and oil are liquids, but sand, rice and dough are all solids. Rice and sand are a bit sneaky because they act like liquids and can be poured, so that makes you think they're liquids. But you probably noticed they don't feel wet — which is a clue that tells you they aren't liquids (although there are some unusual liquids, like mercury, that don't follow this rule). Each individual grain of rice and sand is a solid because it keeps the same shape. The shape of the grains does not change in the way that molecules in a liquid change shape, so rice and sand are solids.

## EVALUATION

How could we have made our experiment more accurate? Instead of using our hands, we could have pressed a paper towel on to the substance to see if any moisture was soaked up. This would be more accurate than testing the substance by feeling with your hand alone.

Ite cool, we've met the sleepy solids, the laid-back liquids and the GASSED gases! Here's a quick reminder of what we learned about them:

★ **The particles in solids are packed tightly together.**

★ **The particles in liquids and gases are packed loosely together.**

★ **Matter can be changed into a different state by melting, boiling, evaporating, condensing or freezing.**

★ **Some solids, such as rice and sand, behave like liquids because they can be poured; however each individual grain is still a solid.**

# CHAPTER 3
# MIX IT UP

## CHAPTER 3

Most of us love a bit of table salt **SPRINKLED ON OUR CHIPS**. **But what actually is table salt?**

You might remember from the intro that table salt is made from two elements: sodium and chlorine! The sodium atom and chlorine atom join together to form a sodium chloride molecule.

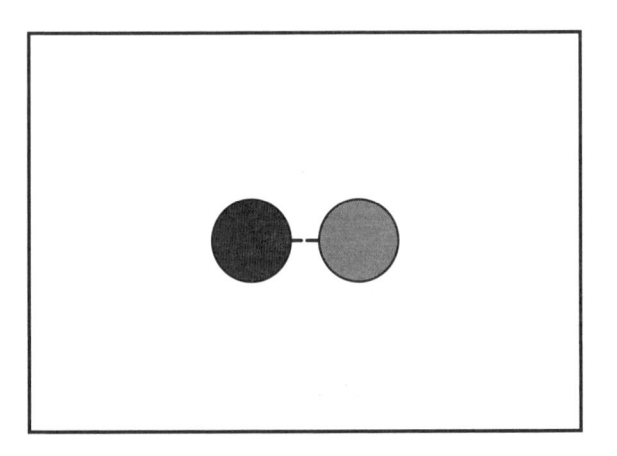

*SODIUM CHLORIDE IS TABLE SALT, INIT!*

**Sodium chloride structure**

**Have you ever taken a teaspoon of salt and mixed it into some water?** After only a few seconds of mixing, the salt begins to disappear! The salt is actually still there though, but it's just **dissolved** into the water.

# MiX iT UP

Dissolved is the scientific way of saying that something has been mixed into a liquid and incorporated into it – which basically means blended together. When you dissolve salt into water, they create a **mixture**.

We call the salt the **solute**, which means the thing being dissolved. And the water is the **solvent**, which is the liquid that the solute is being dissolved in. When a solute is dissolved into a solvent, they form a **solution.** A solution is a type of mixture. You get me? For example, sodium chloride mixed into water creates a sodium chloride solution.

The salt and the water do not chemically join together – they just mix with each other, a bit like two couples going on a double date. After the date is over, the sodium stays with the chlorine in sodium chloride, and the oxygen stays with the hydrogen in $H_2O$. So a mixture is when substances are combined together but not chemically joined (as in, there is no chemical bond between them).

# SODIUM

### CHARACTERISTICS

**A little unpredictable**
(Very reactive/explosive!)

**But also a softie**
(This metal is soft and squishy at room temperature.)

**Star student**
(Sodium is shiny.)

**Hates swimming**
(Will explode in water!)

### LOVES
**Hanging out with chlorine**

### GOOD AT
**Getting loose!**
(Sodium loosens up and melts into a liquid at 98°Celsius – most metals melt at over 1,000° Celsius.)

# CHLORINE

### CHARACTERISTICS

- 😃 **Super excited** (Chlorine is a gas at room temperature.)
- ✨ **Always looks clean and fresh** (Chlorine is used in cleaning products.)
- 💧 **Loves swimming** (Also used in swimming pools to keep the water clean!)

### LOVES 😃😃
Hanging out with **sodium**

### GOOD AT
**Bringing vibes and energy** (Chlorine gas bounces around everywhere.)

## CHAPTER 3

## WHY DOES SALT DISSOLVE IN WATER?

**LEVEL UP**

Right, now we're going to go into **A LiKKLE BiT** more detail about what happens when you mix sodium chloride with $H_2O$.

A sodium chloride molecule is made from two atoms: sodium and chlorine. Sodium and chlorine always stay together – cos they're a couple, init. They're chemically bonded to each other.

$H_2O$ is made from two different atoms as well, two hydrogen and one oxygen atom. Hydrogen and oxygen are like another couple that are chemically bonded together. So we have two couples: sodium chloride and $H_2O$. They love to hang out and mix with each other.

When they mix, the water causes the sodium chloride molecule to split into two and dissolve into the water. When it splits, it turns into separate sodium and chlorine particles.

But why does water cause sodium chloride to split? In an $H_2O$ molecule, the hydrogen particles have a **positive charge** and the oxygen has a **negative charge**. And in a sodium chloride molecule, sodium

# MiX iT UP

has a positive charge and chlorine has
a negative charge.

You might be thinking, where do the positive and negative charges come from? Well – you know how I said atoms are a tiny piece of matter? There are actually some even tinier particles inside atoms called **electrons**, **protons** and **neutrons**. Electrons have a negative charge; protons have a positive charge; and neutrons have no charge. An atom with more protons than electrons will have a positive charge, and an atom with more electrons that protons will have a negative charge. (This is advanced-level science stuff that you don't need to stress about too much til you're older, fam!)

So anyway – the negatively charged oxygen acts like a magnet and pulls the sodium away from chlorine. And the positively charged hydrogen pulls the chlorine away from sodium.

This force that pulls the sodium and chlorine particles apart is called an **electrostatic force**.

Once they've been pulled apart, the sodium and chlorine become separate particles surrounded

## CHAPTER 3

by water. The salt (sodium chloride) has now been dissolved in water ($H_2O$), so it seems to disappear!

So, imagine that sodium has wandered off for a bit to chat with oxygen, and chlorine is getting on really well with hydrogen. BUT they always come back to their couples.

OK, so how can we separate out the sodium chloride from the water? There are actually a couple of ways we can do this:

## SEPARATING A MIXTURE

**1.** We could leave the saltwater mixture on a windowsill for a couple of days and wait for the water to evaporate into a gas out of the mixture.

**2.** We could boil the mixture in a saucepan and get rid of the water.

Both of these options will remove all of the water from the mixture and leave behind only the solid salt. The salt forms crystals as the water is removed from the mixture. This process is known as **crystallization**.

**DIFFICULTY LEVEL:**
Come On Now ⚡⚡🔥

# EXPERIMENT 5: CRYSTALLIZATION

OK — so let's test out these two different methods and compare our results. We want to find out which separation method makes the biggest salt crystals.

> **Ask a grown-up to help you with this one!**

Ite, cool, so first we need a hypothesis, init — what do we think is going to happen? I think that the evaporation method will make bigger salt crystals than the boiling method.

Let's test it and find out. Here's our equipment list:
- ★ 100ml warm water
- ★ three glasses
- ★ around six tablespoons of table salt (sodium chloride)
- ★ a tablespoon
- ★ some string
- ★ a pair of goggles
- ★ a saucepan
- ★ a hob
- ★ a teaspoon
- ★ a ruler

## EVAPORATION METHOD

1. Pour 50ml of warm water into a glass.

2. Add one tablespoon of salt and stir it in.

3. Stir until all of the salt has dissolved and the water is clear.

4. Add more salt and stir until no more salt will dissolve.

5. Place one end of a piece of string into the bottom of the glass and let the other end hang on the outside of the glass.

6. Leave the glass on a windowsill for a few days until the water has evaporated and crystals have formed on the string.

## BOILING METHOD

1. Repeat steps 1–4 and prepare the second glass of saltwater mixture.

2. Put your goggles on in case any water splashes out of the saucepan.

3. Pour the mixture into a saucepan.

4. Boil the mixture on the hob until all of the water has been removed.

5. Once the saucepan has cooled, collect the salt crystals at the bottom with a teaspoon and place into a dry glass. Keep them safe until the crystals have formed from the evaporated mixture.

When we have our salt crystals from both the evaporated mixture and boiled mixture, we can compare their sizes. **Which crystals are bigger?**

Measure both sets of crystals with your ruler. (They might be quite small, so you'll need to use millimetres!).

# RESULTS

Write down your observations and record your results.

_____

_____

_____

Maybe they look a bit like this:

| METHOD | SIZE OF SALT CRYSTAL (MM) |
|---|---|
| Evaporation | 4 |
| Boiling | 1 |

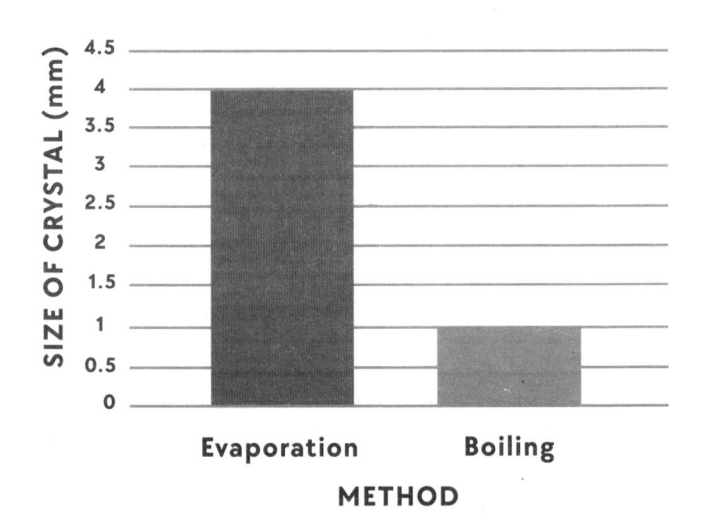

## CONCLUSION

The evaporation method made bigger salt crystals than the boiling method — so our hypothesis was correct! We can conclude that evaporation creates bigger salt crystals than boiling. That's because when you remove the water slowly, the salt crystals have more time to grow.

## EVALUATION

How could we make our results even more accurate? Well, instead of measuring the amount of salt that goes into the water with a tablespoon, we could use some scales instead. Scales weigh more accurately and will allow us to use the exact same amount of salt for each mixture. We could also repeat the experiment and see if we get the same results to make it more precise.

CHAPTER 3

# IT'S SIEVING

Ite, cool, so that's how we separate salt from water, but what if we wanted to separate two solids with different-sized particles? Like, for example, separating sand from stones. We couldn't use the evaporation or boiling method to separate them because they're both solids. Instead, we would have to **sieve** them.

Sieving is actually a really simple process.

You see that mesh wire with a handle that grown-ups use for cooking? That's a sieve.

When you wash food inside a sieve, all of the water runs through the likkle gaps at the bottom.

## MiX iT UP

We can use this same sieve to separate sand from stones.

If we put a mixture of sand and stones into a sieve and shake it, all of the sand will fall through the gaps at the bottom of the sieve because the grains of sand are small. But the stones will not be able to fit through the gaps in the sieve because they are too large. The stones end up left in the sieve while the sand falls through, so they're now separated! Done know, come on!

So what we're going to do is get some dried, long-grain rice and some caster sugar, then mix them together. We're then going to separate the mixture by sieving.

What's your hypothesis for the experiment? Will the sugar or the rice be left in the sieve? Let's find out.

**DIFFICULTY LEVEL:**
Simple Ting

# EXPERIMENT 6: SEPARATING SOLIDS

The equipment that we need for this experiment is:
- ★ half a cup of long-grain rice
- ★ half a cup of caster sugar
- ★ two plastic containers
- ★ spoon
- ★ sieve

## METHOD

1. Measure out half a cup of rice and pour it into one of the plastic containers.

2. Take half a cup of sugar and pour it into the container with the rice.

3. Mix them together well with a spoon.

4. Pour the mixture into the sieve with the other container underneath to catch any falling grains.

5. Shake the mixture in the sieve until the rice and sugar have separated out.

# RESULTS

Now it's time to record your results. Write down which solid stayed in the sieve and which one fell through the holes into the container underneath. Was your hypothesis correct?

**Answer the questions below:**

Why did the grains of rice stay in the sieve?

_____

_____

Why did the grains of sugar fall through the sieve?

_____

_____

# EVALUATION

How could you improve this experiment next time?

_____

_____

_____

## CHAPTER 3

## FILTRATION

OK, so we know how to separate salt that's been dissolved in water, and how to separate two solids with different-sized particles. But what about a solid that *hasn't* been dissolved in the water? Like for example, sand in water.

Sand doesn't dissolve in water like salt does – it just sinks to the bottom. As the sand can't dissolve, we say that it's **insoluble** in water. Insoluble just means that it can't dissolve. Sodium chloride can dissolve, so we say that it's **soluble** in water.

To remove the sand from the mixture, we would need to use a method called **filtration**. Filtration is when you filter a mixture by passing it through a piece of paper with tiny holes, so that all of the water runs through. The sand particles are too large to pass through the holes in the filter paper, so they are collected on its surface. The sand that's left behind is called the **residue** and the water that passes through the filter paper is called the **filtrate**.

# MiX iT UP

Like sieving, filtering involves separating two substances from a mixture according to their size. Filter paper has much smaller holes than a sieve, so we can use it to separate out tiny particles that would go through the sieve. Sieving is the method we use to separate solids, and filtering is used to separate a liquid and an insoluble solid.

ITE, BOOM! WE'VE DONE AN EVAPORATION AND SIEVING EXPERIMENT, SO NOW IT'S TIME FOR A FILTRATION TING.

**DIFFICULTY LEVEL:** Come On Now

# EXPERIMENT 7: FILTRATION STATION

We're going to create a mixture and then separate it using filtration. First thing we need is a mixture, init, so we're going to get some sand and water and mix them together. Next, we're going to filter the mixture using filter paper.

What we need now is a hypothesis. I think that the water will pass through the filter paper but the sand will not. Let's test it!

The equipment that we'll need is:
- ★ measuring jug
- ★ 200ml water
- ★ two glasses
- ★ two tablespoons sand
- ★ funnel
- ★ coffee filter paper (available to buy at large supermarkets)

# METHOD

1. First, measure out 200ml of water and pour it into one of the glasses.

2. Then take two tablespoons of sand and mix it in with the water.

3. The next thing to do is put the funnel into the other glass and fold the piece of filter paper into a cone shape (you might need an adult to help you).

4. Place the filter paper into the funnel and pour the mixture from the other glass into it.

5. As the water is filtering through the filter paper, look at the colour of the water. Is the water still cloudy from the sand? Take a look at the filter paper and see if any sand was collected in there.

## RESULTS

As the mixture is poured through the filter paper, the sand is removed and the water is allowed to pass through into the glass. We'll be able to see that the filter paper contains the sand residue. When we look into the glass, we'll see clear water that no longer contains sand.

## CONCLUSION

We hypothesized that the water would be able to pass through the filter paper but the sand would not. Our results showed that the sand was collected in the filter paper as residue and the water passed through the filter paper into the glass as the filtrate. We can conclude that our hypothesis was correct!

## EVALUATION

Is there anything you would have done differently in this experiment? Maybe you could have taken a picture of the cloudy mixture before and the clear water afterwards? Using photos to compare the difference instead of just looking at the mixture would make our experiment more accurate.

# MiX iT UP

Let's look at a few questions on filtration. Below we have a list of different mixtures that were filtered. For each mixture, can you work out what the filtrate and residue are? Once you're done, take a look at p.200 for the answers.

| COMBINATIONS | FILTRATE | RESIDUE |
|---|---|---|
| **Rice and oil** | | |
| **Water and soil** | | |
| **Cereal and milk** | | |

**BOOM!** So in this chapter we've learned how to mix things up and separate them out again.

Remember, a mixture is when substances are combined together but not chemically joined, like when we mixed sand into water. We could easily separate the sand from the water by filtering it.

A solution is a type of mixture where one substance is dissolved in another. Solutions can be separated by boiling or evaporating the mixture, which removes the water (solvent) and leaves behind the solid (solute).

Cool, so let's recap some of the other key points from this chapter:

★ A mixture contains two or more different substances that are not chemically joined. It can be a mixture of two solids (rice and sugar), two liquids (water and oil), a liquid and a soluble solid (water and sodium chloride) or a liquid and an insoluble solid (water and sand).

★ We call the substance that's being dissolved the solute, and the liquid that it's being dissolved in the solvent.

★ We can separate larger-sized solids from smaller ones by sieving them to allow small ones to fall through the gaps, and collect the larger ones.

★ We can separate an insoluble (undissolved) solid, like sand, from water using filter paper to capture the solid and allow the water to pass through.

★ We can separate solutions through evaporation and boiling.

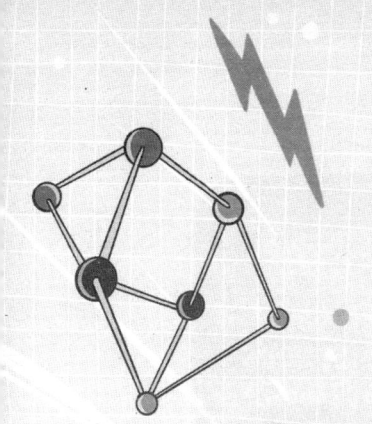

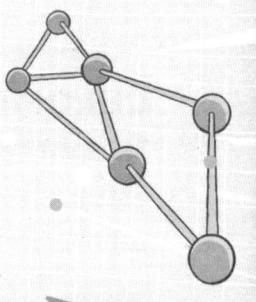

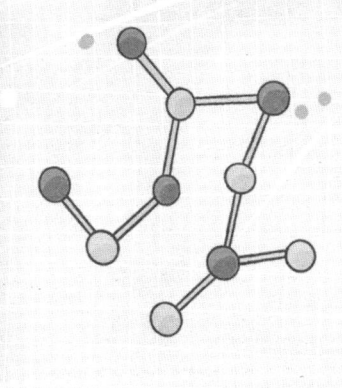

# CHAPTER 4
# LET'S SPLIT

# CHAPTER 4

> OK – MAN'S GOT MIXTURES DOWN NOW – SO WE'RE GONNA LOOK AT SOME EVEN MORE ADVANCED WAYS TO SEPARATE THEM. THESE METHODS SOUND HARD BUT THEY'RE ACTUALLY NOT THAT MAD, TRUST ME!

## CHROMA-WHAT-NOW?

The next separation method we're gonna talk about is chromatography. Let me say that again:

> KRO – MA – TOH – GRA – FEE

You might be thinking this is to do with some high-tech chemicals but actually, nah. It's to do with something you use every day in school.

# LET'S SPLIT

We've all been there – sat in lessons waiting for the bell and you're messing around with your pen then **BOOM!** Your pen explodes. Ink splattered all over your hands, desk – even on your shirt! **But as you try to scrub off those blotches from your skin, have you ever wondered what this stuff is even made of?**

Pen ink is a mixture that contains something we call **pigments**. Pigments are basically pure colour: they are substances that are able to change the colour of reflected light, so that it appears as a certain shade to the human eye. For example, green ink contains a mixture of yellow and blue pigments to make green. Most pigments are **inorganic** (or human-made) but there are some pigments in nature too.

**Chromatography** allows us to see all the different-coloured pigments within an ink droplet, just by using water! Some of the pigments are more soluble than others, which means they dissolve more easily, so the water can carry them further. This splits the ink into a rainbow of different-coloured pigments.

**DIFFICULTY LEVEL:**
Come On Now ⚡⚡

# EXPERIMENT 8: CHROMATOGRAPHY

Ite, **BOOM!** We're gonna do a likkle experiment. We're gonna separate the pigments in some ink and see which pigment is the most soluble.

SO JUST LIKE LAST TIME, WE NEED OUR HYPOTHESIS, iNiT - OTHERWISE WE DON'T KNOW WHAT TO LOOK OUT FOR. I'M EXPECTING TO SEE THE YELLOW PIGMENT DISSOLVE THE FASTEST, SO LET'S TEST iT AND SEE WAGWAN.

This is our equipment list:
- ★ a small piece of paper
- ★ a green felt-tip pen
- ★ a pair of tweezers
- ★ a small glass of tap water
- ★ a ruler

## METHOD

1. Draw a round dot on the small bit of paper with the green felt-tip pen.

2. Grab your tweezers.

3. Grip your piece of paper with the tweezers and hold it over the glass of water so the edge of the paper is just touching the surface of the water.

4. You'll start seeing the water travel from the glass and up along the paper until it passes over the ink.

5. Once it reaches the ink, it should carry the pigments along with it.

6. The pigment that has the most solubility will be carried further up the paper by the water.

7. The pigment with the least solubility will be left behind and won't be carried up as far.

**OK - GO AHEAD AND TRY THAT! PIGMENT SETTINGS.**

8. Use your ruler to measure the distance from the ink circle to where each pigment stopped.

# RESULTS

Now that our green ink has been separated into two pigments, which one turned out to be the most soluble? Your results might look something like this.

| PIGMENT | DISTANCE TRAVELLED (MM) |
|---|---|
| Blue | 30 |
| Yellow | 25 |

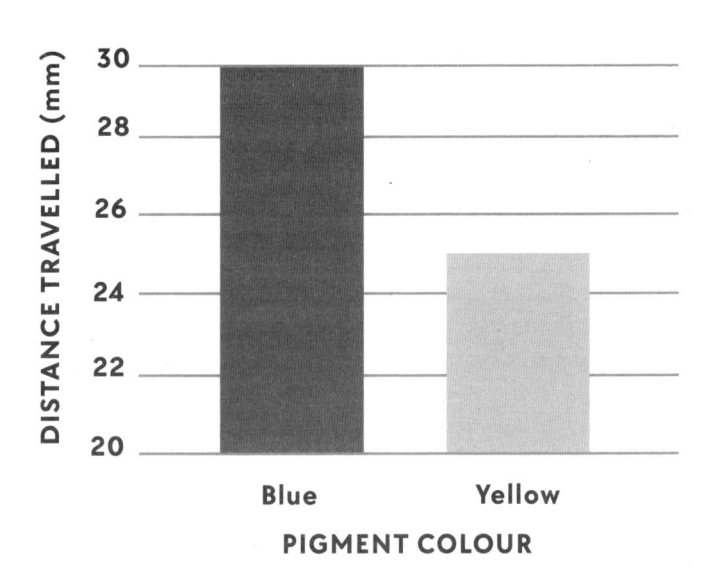

**PIGMENT COLOUR**

## CONCLUSION

**Did yellow travel the furthest along the paper?** Nah, this time our hypothesis was incorrect! We can conclude that blue pigment is more soluble in water than yellow pigment because it travelled further. The yellow pigment is less soluble in water. The reason why the pigment with higher solubility will travel further is because it has a stronger electrostatic force of attraction with the water. It's as if there's a strong magnet pulling the blue pigment along. The yellow pigment is pulled along by the same kind of force, but it's not quite as strong, so it doesn't travel as far.

## EVALUATION

So how could we improve this experiment to make it more precise? Well, we could repeat it more than once and make sure that we get similar results each time. **But how would we improve the accuracy?** We could measure the amount of water we put into the glass. This would make our results more accurate. We could also make sure that we used the same type of green pen for each test.

## CHAPTER 4

# DISTILL AND CHILL

Ite, so **BOOM!** In the last chapter, we learned how to separate salt from water through evaporation and boiling. But we were left with just the salt crystals, while the water turned into a gas and disappeared. So what if we wanted to get the liquid water back?

To do this, we're gonna use a process called **distillation**. This is similar to evaporation because the first step is to heat the liquid water so that it changes into a gas.

But distillation doesn't stop there, because after the water has been evaporated into a gas, we flip things back to square one by changing it back to a liquid again through condensation of the gas molecules. This is done by chilling things out and bringing the water's temperature right back down so that it becomes a liquid and we can collect it.

Man's gonna show you how this works now with a simple experiment.

**DIFFICULTY LEVEL:**
Come On Now

# EXPERIMENT 9: DISTILLATION

> **Ask a grown-up to help you with this one!**

First, we're gonna heat up some salty water in a pan with a lid, then see what happens when we reduce the heat. What do you think will happen to the saltwater? Write down your hypothesis.

Equipment list:
- ★ a pair of goggles
- ★ a measuring jug
- ★ 50ml water
- ★ one tablespoon of fine table salt
- ★ a teaspoon
- ★ a metal pot with a lid
- ★ a hob
- ★ oven gloves
- ★ empty glass
- ★ a spatula

# METHOD

1. Start by putting your goggles on.

2. Measure out 50ml of water in your measuring jug and then add your tablespoon of salt.

3. Stir the mixture until all of the salt dissolves and it becomes a solution.

4. Test the salt taste by taking a teaspoonful of water out and tasting it. (This part is optional! Yuck, that's bare salty.)

5. Add your saltwater solution to a pot with a lid. (This works best with a pot with a wide base.)

6. Close the lid and bring the saltwater solution to a boil on a high heat.

> **!** Make sure you and your grown-up keep an eye on the boiling water and take the pan off the heat just before all the water has disappeared. This will stop the pan from burning.

7. Once you see some steam starting to escape, let it boil for another minute or two before reducing the heat to low.

8. With your oven gloves on, carefully lift the lid and expose its underside — you should see that water droplets have formed.

9. Gently move the lid and hold it over your empty glass.

10. Grab your spatula and scrape the water droplets downwards into your glass.

11. If you don't collect enough water on the first try, then reheat the pot of saltwater solution. Repeat the steps until you've collected enough water for a drink of clean, non-salty water!

## RESULTS

Ite, **BOOM!** So you've taken a sip from your freshly distilled glass of water and made sure the distillation process worked, init.
**Do you notice how the salt taste has completely disappeared and you're left with a crystal-clear glass of water?** Purity settings.

**DONE KNOW.**

Where has that salty taste gone? Well, when the salty water in the pot was heated, the water evaporated into vapour and floated around inside the pot. As soon as the water vapour touched the cold pot lid, it condensed back into a liquid. Meanwhile, the salt was left behind at the bottom of the pot as a solid.

## CONCLUSION

Was your hypothesis correct? If you wrote down that the salt water would evaporate when heated and condense when cooled, nice one, fam!

## EVALUATION

Is there anything we could do differently in this experiment? Well, we could also use our measuring jug to see how much water was collected at the end of the experiment. Is it the same as what we had at the start, or a bit less? Why do you think that is?

LET'S SPLIT

## DISTILLATION SALVATION

Distillation isn't just a cool science experiment – it can literally save lives. Let me explain . . .

LEVEL UP

We know that water is essential for human survival, and more than 96% of the planet's liquid is seawater. **Seawater is still water, right?**

Well, imagine you've crash-landed on a deserted island and you're feeling thirsty.

Some people might be asking,

> WHAT'S THE PROBLEM? YOU'RE SURROUNDED BY WATER, JUST DRINK THAT, INIT?

Unless you want to experience severe dizziness and exhaustion, take my advice and leave the salt water alone.

A bit of salt in your food is all good, but the human body can only manage so much before the kidneys – special organs that remove waste material from your blood – need to start filtering it out through your pee. Seawater contains mad amounts of salt –

## CHAPTER 4

about three times more than what's in your blood, in fact.

So in order for your body to flush out the extra salt, your body would have to release more water to carry it out. In other words, the more saltwater you drink, the thirstier and more dehydrated you'll become. **MAD TING STILL!**

But if you were to remove the salt from the ocean water using distillation, it would be safe to drink. Distillation can also be used to clean muddy and contaminated water. If you heat muddy water to 100° Celsius in a contained space, the water will boil away, leaving the mud behind as a solid. You can then collect the pure, clear water (just like you did with the pan lid).

Distillation is often used in emergencies and natural disasters as a safe way to purify water when there's no fresh water available to drink. And in some countries where there isn't much fresh water, solar-powered distillation – a method of distillation that's powered by heat from the sun – is being used to make water that's safe to drink.

## LET'S SPLIT

> JUST THiNK OF ALL THE YOUNG G'S AROUND THE WORLD WHO DON'T HAVE ACCESS TO CLEAN WATER. DiSTiLLATiON iS A GAME-CHANGER!

# FRACTIONAL DISTILLATION

What we have to understand is that there are levels to this distillation thing. There is an even more precise version of distillation called **fractional distillation**. Instead of separating a solvent and a solute, this process can be used to separate two liquids that have different boiling points.

A **boiling point** is the temperature at which a liquid decides . . .

> NAH I'VE HAD ENOUGH OF THiS HEAT. I'M OUT.

. . . and starts to evaporate.

## CHAPTER 4

Different liquids have different boiling points. For example, as we all know, water will boil at 100° Celsius, but olive oil has a much higher boiling point at 180° Celsius.

*OLIVE OIL CAN FIRM THAT HEAT FOR A BIT LONGER BEFORE TAPPING OUT!*

If a mixture of oil and water was boiled to 100° Celsius, the water would evaporate, leaving the oil behind.

## LET'S SPLIT

> **!** Don't try this at home, though, as the oil gets mad hot and it could jump out of the pan and burn you!

Here are some more examples of different boiling points:

| LIQUID | BOILING POINT (DEGREES CELSIUS) |
|---|---|
| Petrol | 35 |
| Ethanol (alcohol) | 78 |
| Water | 100 |
| Oil | 180 |
| Mercury | 356 |

**WOAH, MERCURY'S BOILING POINT IS CRAZY HIGH! MERCURY IS THE ONLY METAL ON EARTH THAT IS LIQUID AT ROOM TEMPERATURE. MAD TING.**

BOOM! In this chapter we levelled up our separation methods and discovered how chromatography, distillation and fractional distillation work. Big tings! Here are the key points we learned:

★ **Chromatography can be used to separate different parts of a mixture using a solvent – for example, using water to separate pigments in ink.**

★ **Distillation can be used to purify a liquid by first evaporating it into a gas and then condensing it back into a liquid.**

★ **Fractional distillation is used to separate liquids that have different boiling points, for example, oil and water.**

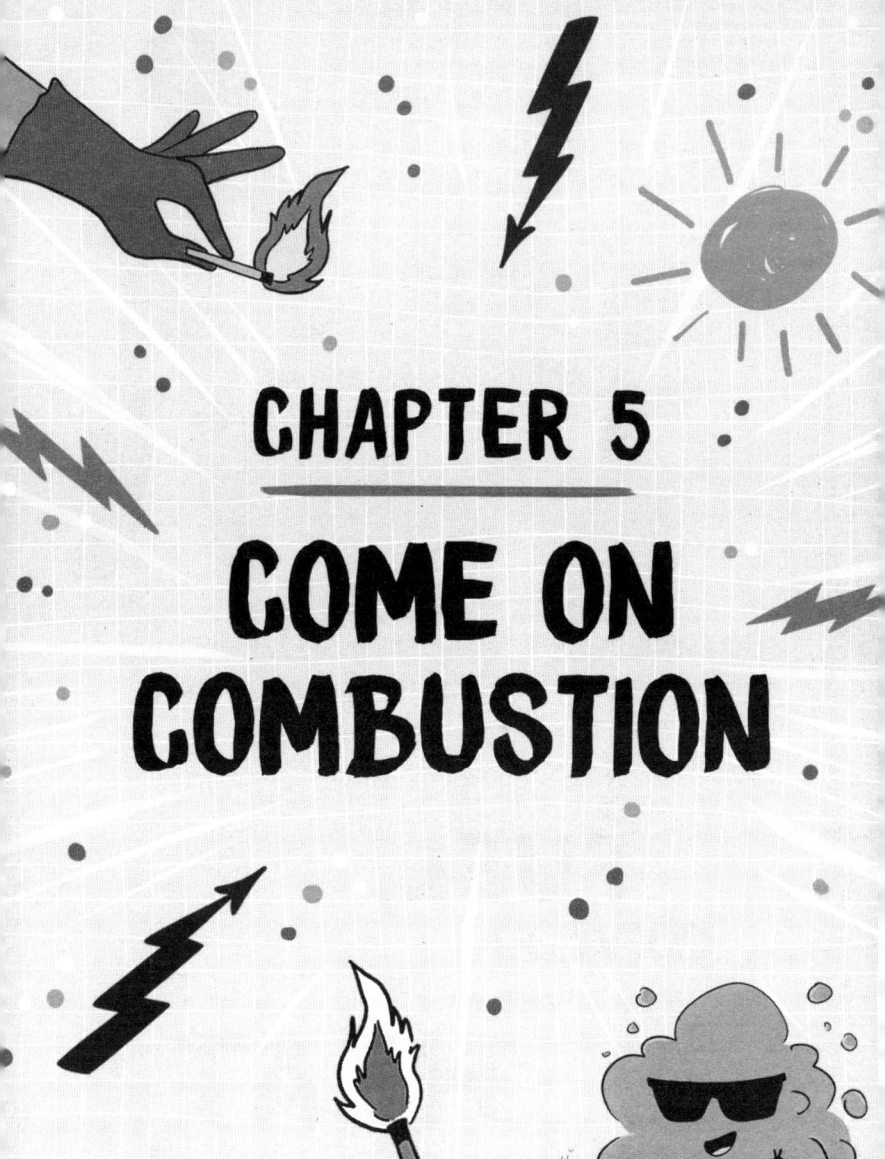

# CHAPTER 5

# COME ON COMBUSTION

## CHAPTER 5

> RIGHT, NOW WE'RE GOING TO GET LIT, LITERALLY.

The scientific word for burning is **combustion**. In order to make something burn, three ingredients are needed. These ingredients are:

# FUEL, OXYGEN and HEAT

Even if just one of these three ingredients is missing, there won't be any combustion.

# COME ON COMBUSTION

## SO WHAT EXACTLY IS A FUEL?

A fuel is a substance that is used to create energy. When fuel is heated, it reacts with oxygen to produce thermal energy (this is the scientific name for heat). Thermal energy has many useful purposes, such as heating our homes, powering our cars and giving us electricity. Some examples of fuels are petrol for cars, gas that heats cookers, and candle wax.

★ **When petrol is burned in a car engine, thermal energy is released. This is turned into mechanical energy (basically, energy that moves or has the potential to move an object), which turns the wheels of the car.**

★ **Burning gas from a cooker gives us thermal energy to cook food.**

★ **Burning a candle also gives us thermal energy and light.**

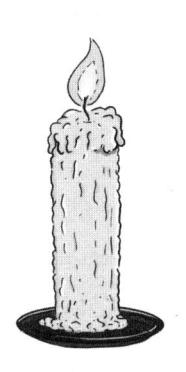

## CHAPTER 5

## OXIDATION – WHAT'S THAT?

OK, so now that we know what fuels are, let's look at where oxygen comes in.

So obviously oxygen is in the air, init, and as we know, fuels react with oxygen when they are heated.

The fuel is oxidized by oxygen when it burns. **Oxidation** just means that the fuel is reacting with the oxygen and they bond together.

YOU GET ME?

Candle wax is a type of fuel made from hydrogen and carbon. When it's burned, the oxygen in the air reacts with carbon from the wax and they bond together to make carbon dioxide.

Carbon (C) + Oxygen ($O_2$) → Carbon dioxide ($CO_2$)

SIMPLE TINGS! THAT'S OXIDATION.

**What about the hydrogen from the wax, though?** The hydrogen also reacts with oxygen in the air and gets oxidized.

# COME ON COMBUSTION

**What do you get when you react hydrogen with oxygen?** Water!

Hydrogen ($H_2$) + Oxygen ($O_2$) $\longrightarrow$ Water ($H_2O$)

When we burn any kind of fuel – in this case, candle wax – two products are made: carbon dioxide and water. The water that's created in this reaction is in the form of water vapour because the heat from the candle evaporates the water into a gas.

## REVERSIBLE AND IRREVERSIBLE CHANGES

*MAD TiNG. DONE KNOW.*

An important thing to know about combustion is that it's an **irreversible change**. An irreversible change is a change that can't be undone.

So far in this book, we've looked at some **reversible changes**, including freezing, evaporating, boiling and mixing. In a reversible change, you can go back to what you had at the start before the change took place. It's like the rewind button on the TV remote.

# CHAPTER 5

For example, if we freeze a cup of water into solid ice, we can easily get the liquid water back by leaving it on a table to melt. The heat from the room would be enough to melt the ice. That's why freezing is a reversible change because we can turn the ice back into a liquid again using heat.

In reversible changes no new products are made. Reversible changes are also called **physical changes** because they often involve a substance changing into a different state, like ice melting to water.

But an irreversible change creates new products that can't be turned back into what they were before the reaction. When we burn candle wax and turn it into carbon dioxide gas and water, can we turn it back into wax after that? Nope, we can't. That's why combustion is an irreversible change.

Another example of an irreversible change is cooking. When you fry an egg, it goes from a liquid to a solid when it touches the hot pan. The heat causes the egg to go from **translucent** (or see-through) to **opaque** (the opposite of see-through!) as it solidifies. There's no way to turn the solid fried egg back into a runny, liquid egg – it's a fried egg forever.

## COME ON COMBUSTION

Irreversible changes are also called **chemical changes**. You can tell if a chemical change is happening because you will usually see some kind of fizzing or colour change, or heat or a gas might be released.

## HEATING AND MIXING

> YOU MIGHT BE THINKING, HOLD UP – SO CAN HEAT CAUSE BOTH REVERSIBLE AND IRREVERSIBLE CHANGES?

That's right – heat causes a reversible change to ice when it is melted, but it can also cause an irreversible change to food when it's cooked. So heat can cause both irreversible and reversible changes depending on what the substance is.

Mixing can also cause both reversible and irreversible changes. Mixing salt with water is a reversible change because we can separate them afterwards, but mixing cement with water is irreversible because it creates solid concrete, which can't be separated again.

OK – now that we know the difference between reversible and irreversible changes, let's get back to combustion!

**DIFFICULTY LEVEL:** Come On Now

# EXPERIMENT 10: OXYGEN IS KEY

> **Ask a grown-up to help you with this one!**

A fuel will never burn without oxygen, no matter how much we heat it. We could heat it to 1,000,000° Celsius and it still wouldn't burn without oxygen. If you don't believe me, we can even do an experiment to prove it. All we need to do is remove the oxygen from a fire and see what effect it has.

**What do you think will happen when we remove the oxygen from a fire?** I think that it will cause the fire to go out. To test this, we're going to need some equipment.

Equipment list:
- ★ a pair of goggles
- ★ a tea light
- ★ matches
- ★ a glass

## METHOD

1. Put your goggles on.

2. Then strike a match and use it to light the tea light.

3. Once the tea light is lit, put the glass over the flame to cover it. **What can you see happening when you cover the flame?**

The flame on the tea light gradually gets smaller and smaller until it eventually goes out. When a flame has gone out, we say that it has been extinguished. To **extinguish** a fire just means to put it out.

## RESULTS

**So why did the flame actually go out?**
When we covered the tea light with the glass, the oxygen supply going to the flame from the air was cut off. The only oxygen that the tea light had to burn was the oxygen left inside the glass. The fuel from the tea light was oxidized by all of the remaining oxygen in the glass. When all of the oxygen in the glass was used up by the tea light, the flame went out.

## CONCLUSION

Was our hypothesis correct? Yeah — we said the fire would go out, and it did!

# OXYGEN

WHEN CARBON AND OXYGEN GET TOGETHER, THEY FORM CARBON DIOXIDE. CARBON DIOXIDE HAS MANY USES – FOR EXAMPLE, IT MAKES THE BUBBLES IN FIZZY DRINKS!

## ♥ CHARACTERISTICS
**Has so many friends they can't keep track of them all** (reacts with many elements).

## LOVES
**Getting lit!** (Oxygen is essential for combustion.) **Hanging out with hydrogen** ($H_2 + O$ = water)

## GOOD AT
**Being the life of the party** (oxygen is essential for life!)

# CARBON

## ☀ CHARACTERISTICS
**Loves summertime and BBQs** (Charcoal is burned for cooking.)

**pretty tough** (carbon is solid at room temperature)

## LOVES 😄😊
**Hanging out with oxygen**
($C + O_2 = CO_2$)

## GOOD AT
**Bringing energy** (because it's a fuel!)

CHAPTER 5

## WHAT ACTUALLY IS A FUEL?

The main types of fuels that we use are **hydrocarbons**. Why are they called hydrocarbons?

> WELL, THE ANSWER IS REALLY EASY! IT'S BECAUSE THEY'RE MADE FROM HYDROGEN AND CARBON ATOMS, INIT.

The simplest type of hydrocarbon is **methane**. Methane is a gas and we can burn it to produce useful thermal energy.

> DID YOU KNOW THAT US HUMANS ACTUALLY PRODUCE METHANE IN OUR BODIES WHEN WE DIGEST FOOD? METHANE IS PASSED THROUGH OUR DIGESTIVE SYSTEM AND RELEASED AS A GAS THROUGH FARTS! BARE STINKY ...

Methane is the simplest hydrocarbon because it's made from only one carbon atom and four hydrogen atoms. The carbon atom has four bonds that stretch out like arms. These four 'arms' or bonds

# COME ON COMBUSTION

of the carbon are chemically bonded with one hydrogen atom each.

This creates a methane molecule. The chemical **formula** for methane is **CH₄** because it contains one carbon atom and four hydrogen atoms.

**CHAPTER 5**

# COMBUSTION CHEMICAL EQUATIONS

Ite cool, it's getting mad. Now we're going to look at an actual **chemical equation** for a combustion reaction using methane as our fuel. An equation just tells us what is made when we add two things together, for example 1 + 1 = 2.

**What's the equation for methane + oxygen though? What is made when methane is burned and oxidized by oxygen?**

**BOOM!** Well, the first thing we need is the chemical formula for methane, which is $CH_4$. Then we need the chemical formula for oxygen gas, which is $O_2$.

All we have to do is add them together like this: $CH_4 + O_2$.

**Can you remember the products made when we burned the candle wax?** The carbon from $CH_4$ (methane – your fuel) reacts and bonds with the oxygen to form $CO_2$, or carbon dioxide. The hydrogen from $CH_4$ reacts and bonds with the oxygen to form $H_2O$, or water.

## COME ON COMBUSTION

So we've just created two products from the combustion of methane with oxygen – these products are carbon dioxide and water.

> DONE KNOW COME ON. COMBUSTION TING.

The full chemical equation for the combustion of methane gas is:
$CH_4 + O_2 \longrightarrow CO_2 + H_2O$.

This can also be written as
Methane + Oxygen $\longrightarrow$ Carbon dioxide + Water.

## DRAWING FUELS

**All right cool, so what do fuels actually look like?** I've got **A LIKKLE CHALLENGE** here for you – we're going to draw the structure of different fuels. Let's start with methane. Trust me – it's going to be easy. So methane has only one carbon atom bonded to four hydrogen atoms. It looks like this:

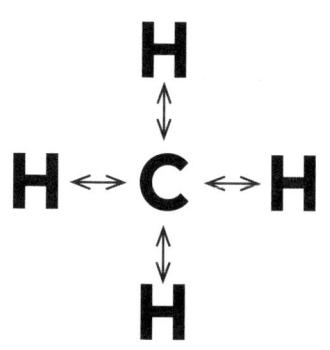

$$\begin{array}{c} H \\ \updownarrow \\ H \leftrightarrow C \leftrightarrow H \\ \updownarrow \\ H \end{array}$$

## CHAPTER 5

The next most complicated hydrocarbon is **ethane**. Now ethane is bare easy; it's just like methane but instead of one carbon atom, it has two carbon atoms bonded to each other. Ethane looks like this:

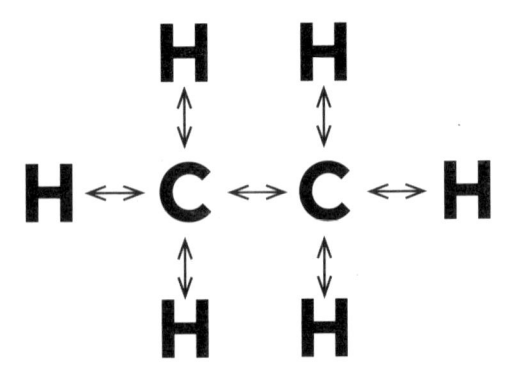

```
        H   H
        ↕   ↕
    H ↔ C ↔ C ↔ H
        ↕   ↕
        H   H
```

So ethane has two carbon atoms and each carbon atom is bonded to three hydrogen atoms.

The next hydrocarbon up from this is **propane**. Now I'm not actually going to draw propane for you – you're going to do this one. But I'll give you a clue. Propane has three carbon atoms in it, and the carbon atoms are linked together in a chain just like how they are in ethane. Each carbon atom is also bonded to hydrogen atoms.

## COME ON COMBUSTION

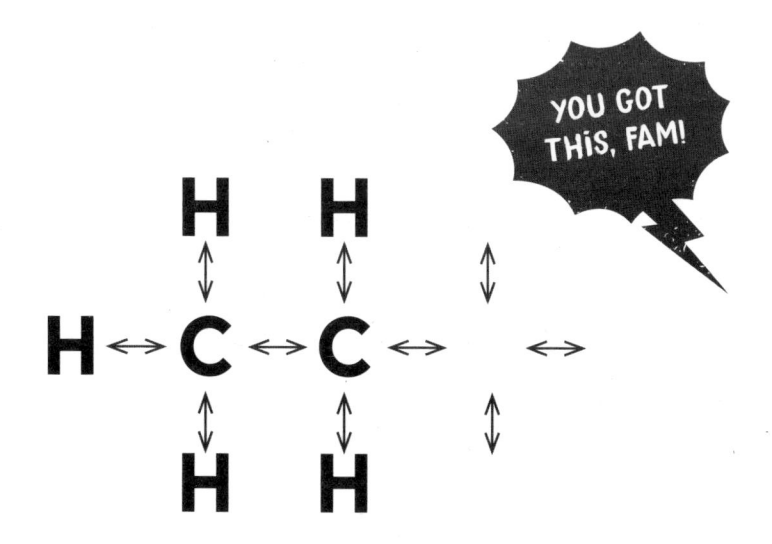

**YOU GOT THIS, FAM!**

```
    H   H
    ↕   ↕   ↕
H ↔ C ↔ C ↔   ↔
    ↕   ↕   ↕
    H   H
```

Once you've had a go at propane, the next one up is **butane**. See if you can draw its structure – I'll give you a clue: it has four carbon atoms!

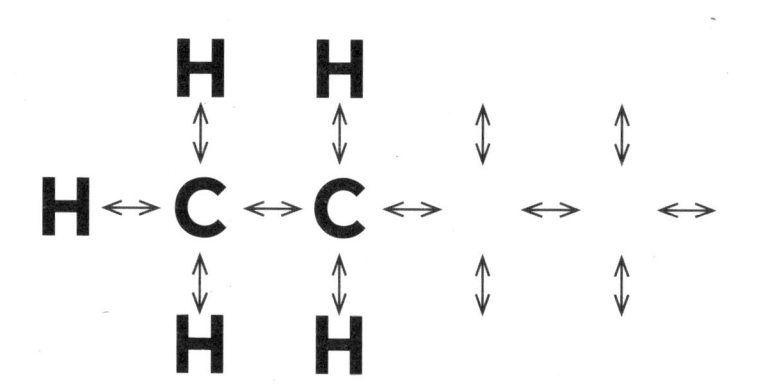

```
    H   H
    ↕   ↕   ↕   ↕
H ↔ C ↔ C ↔   ↔   ↔
    ↕   ↕   ↕   ↕
    H   H
```

# HYDROGEN

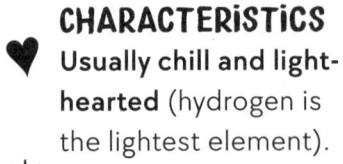

### ♥ CHARACTERISTICS
Usually chill and light-hearted (hydrogen is the lightest element).

But say the wrong thing and it can get **EXPLOSIVE** (hydrogen is very flammable).

### LOVES 😄😄
Oxygen
($H_2 + O_2$ = water)

### GOOD AT
Athletics – running and jumping (because hydrogen is *light* on its feet!)

## COME ON COMBUSTION

## SOOT? NEVER HEARD OF IT

**You see when people sweep chimneys or fireplaces, what's all that black powdery stuff that comes out?** That's called soot. Now soot is basically just pure carbon atoms. These carbon atoms come from the fuel that was being burned. The scientific name for soot is particulate carbon.

Remember, most common fuels are hydrocarbons made from hydrogen and carbon, and the oxygen reacts with them during combustion. The oxygen turns carbon into carbon dioxide. What happens if there isn't enough oxygen, though?

Well, if there's not enough oxygen, then not all of the carbon from the fuel will be oxidized into carbon dioxide. As a result, there will be some leftover carbon atoms that weren't oxidized.

## CHAPTER 5

*DONE KNOW.*

This is why we see the black soot in chimneys, because some of the carbon was left behind from the fuel and didn't react with the oxygen to form carbon dioxide. When there isn't enough oxygen, it's called **incomplete combustion**.

The reason why it's called incomplete combustion is because not all of the fuel was burned. Now with an incomplete combustion reaction, we actually get a third product, which is **carbon monoxide.**

What's that? The 'mono' in the name is a clue – instead of two oxygen atoms like you have in carbon dioxide, carbon monoxide has just one oxygen atom. Carbon monoxide is made in incomplete combustion cos there's less oxygen for the carbon to bond with.

Sometimes if there's really little oxygen, you just get left with carbon atoms – or soot – or you might get a mixture of both carbon monoxide *and* soot.

So incomplete combustion makes carbon dioxide, carbon monoxide and water, and sometimes soot. **Complete combustion** makes only carbon dioxide and water. That's the difference between complete combustion and incomplete combustion.

**DIFFICULTY LEVEL:**
Come On Now

# EXPERIMENT 11: MAKING SOOT

**Ask a grown-up to help you with this one!**

Ite cool, so right here I've got a likkle experiment. We're going to make some soot using incomplete combustion. Obviously we need some scientific equipment first, init.

Equipment list:
- ★ a pair of goggles
- ★ gloves
- ★ a candle
- ★ a candleholder
- ★ matches
- ★ a spoon

**! Be careful as the dripping wax will be mad hot!**

## METHOD

1. Put your goggles and gloves on. Make sure your candle is securely positioned in your candleholder.

2. Then light the candle using a match.

3. Put the bowl of the spoon at the centre of the candle's flame and leave it there for a few seconds. What can you see happening?

## RESULTS

The underside of the spoon's bowl is being coated with a layer of soot. This soot is tiny particles of carbon. Why is the soot appearing on the spoon, though?

Well, some of the carbon from the wax reacted with the oxygen in the air during burning to produce carbon dioxide. However, some of the carbon from the wax did not react with the oxygen in the air, so it was left behind as solid carbon particles (soot). This is incomplete combustion. Some of the solid carbon particles then built up on the spoon, turning it black.

## CONCLUSION

We said we were gonna make soot — so the experiment happened as we predicted. Boom!

## EVALUATION

How could we make this more accurate and precise? We could have timed the number of seconds it took for the soot to form and then repeated the experiment a few times to see if we got similar results..

Ite, BOOM! So we've got LIT with combustion and got to know a bit more about our guys oxygen, hydrogen and carbon.

**What are our key points from this chapter?**

★ For combustion to happen we need heat, fuel and oxygen.

★ Fuel is a substance that we burn to produce useful thermal energy, or heat. The main types of fuels are hydrocarbons – made from hydrogen and carbon atoms.

★ Oxidation is the process of oxygen reacting with a substance. During combustion, oxygen reacts with a fuel to produce carbon dioxide and water.

★ Irreversible changes (also known as chemical changes) are changes that cannot be undone. In irreversible changes, new products are created that can't be turned back into the original products.

- ★ Reversible changes are changes that can be undone. Reversible changes usually involve changing from one state to another, such as water freezing into ice.

- ★ The products of complete combustion are carbon dioxide and water.

- ★ Incomplete combustion happens when there isn't enough oxygen for the fuel to fully burn, which produces carbon monoxide, carbon dioxide and water (and sometimes particulate carbon, or soot).

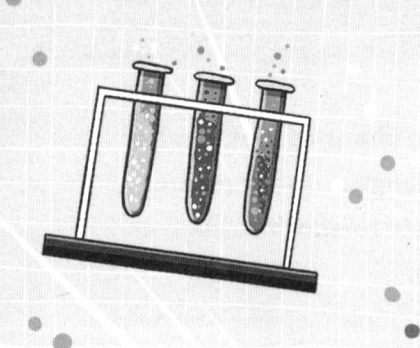

# CHAPTER 6

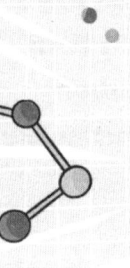

# I CAN'T ALKALIE

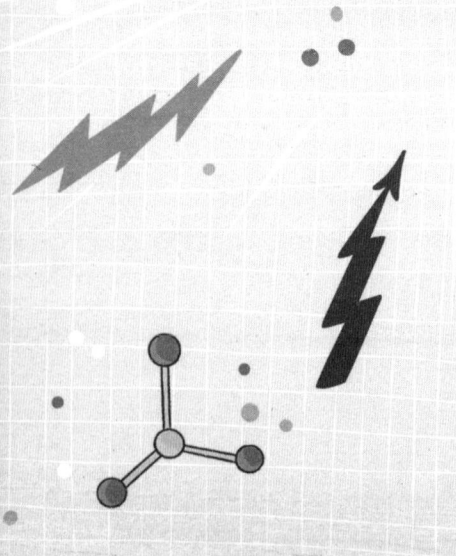

# I CAN'T ALKALIE

## ACID, ALKALI OR NEUTRAL?

Ite, BOOM! Every type of liquid in the world can be put into one of three groups: acids, alkalis and neutral.

**LEVEL UP**

An example of an **acid** is lemon juice – bare zesty. If you've ever bitten into a lemon then you'll notice that it tastes really sour, because it's acidic.

An example of an **alkali** is washing-up liquid – **DiSH SOAP TiNG, iNiT.**

If you've ever ended up with soap in your mouth then you would have tasted the bitterness, *yuck!*

> ALLOW iT, FAM. THAT BiTTERNESS iS BECAUSE iT'S AN ALKALi.

Acids are like the popular kids who always look sharp and love to socialize all the time. Alkalis are the complete opposite of acids – they're super laid-back and carefree but they'll also burn you if they get the chance.

CHAPTER 6

## NEUTRALIZATION

When they're mixed together in equal amounts, acids and alkalis **neutralize** each other. That basically means they cancel each other out. So when those popular kids pick a fight with those laid-back kids, no one is winning that fight.

We can identify acids and alkalis using **a pH indicator**. Indicators will tell us whether a liquid is acidic, alkaline or neutral. The liquid changes colour when the indicator is added, and the colour that it turns tells us whether it is an acid or alkali.

REMEMBER: A COLOUR CHANGE TELLS US THAT AN IRREVERSIBLE OR CHEMICAL CHANGE IS TAKING PLACE.

> THE INDICATOR IS A BIT LIKE THE TEACHER WHO CAN TELL STRAIGHT AWAY WHAT KINDA MOOD THEIR CLASS IS IN!

Acids and alkalis come in different strengths and the colour change will also tell us how strong they are.

★ **If the acid or alkali is weak, we say it's diluted.**

★ **If the acid or alkali is strong, we say it's concentrated.**

We measure how acidic or alkaline something is by using the **pH scale**.

## THE PH SCALE

Each colour on the pH scale has a different number. To find out the pH number of a substance, you would:

★ **Test your substance with an indicator.**

★ **Check what colour the indicator turns.**

## CHAPTER 6

- ★ Find the number on the chart that matches that colour.

- ★ If the liquid has a pH number between 0 and 6 then it's an acid.

- ★ If it has a pH number between 8 and 14 then it's an alkali.

Right in the middle we have pH 7, which is neither acidic or alkaline – it's neutral.

Water has a pH of 7 – neutral settings, you get me? In a fight between acids and alkalis, water would be the neutral one trying to chill everyone out. The lower the pH number, the more acidic the liquid is. The higher the pH number, the more alkaline the liquid is.

Our stomachs have hydrochloric acid inside, and we use it to digest food. This acid has a pH number of 2, so it's a strong acid. Coffee, on the other hand, has a pH of 5, so it's a much weaker acid. Washing-up liquid has a pH of 8, so it's an alkali.

**DIFFICULTY LEVEL:** Big Science

# EXPERIMENT 12: MAKING A RED-CABBAGE INDICATOR

### Ask a grown-up to help you with this one!

One natural indicator that we can use is red-cabbage juice. When you put red-cabbage juice into a liquid, the liquid changes colour. We're going to make our own red-cabbage juice and then use it to test acids and alkalis.

Equipment list:
- ★ a pair of goggles
- ★ a kitchen knife
- ★ half a red cabbage
- ★ a chopping board
- ★ a jug
- ★ a kettle
- ★ a bowl
- ★ a sieve
- ★ five glasses
- ★ 50ml each of white distilled vinegar, lemon juice, soapy water, water

Lemon juice and vinegar: acidic or alkaline? I think acidic, to be honest. And what about the water and soapy water? Write down your hypothesis!

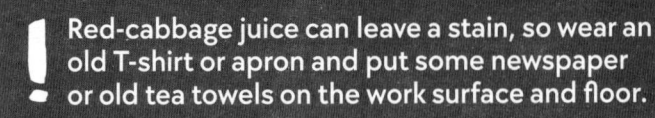

> ! Red-cabbage juice can leave a stain, so wear an old T-shirt or apron and put some newspaper or old tea towels on the work surface and floor.

## METHOD

Put your goggles on (we don't want any acids or alkalis getting in our eyes!).

**Prepare red-cabbage indicator:**

1. Use your kitchen knife to cut up the red cabbage on a chopping board. (You might need an adult to help you!)

2. Put the red cabbage into a jug.

3. Fill and boil the kettle.

4. Pour the hot, boiled water into the jug until it covers the red cabbage. (Depending what size of jug you're using, you may need a different amount of water to cover the red cabbage.)

5. Wait for ten minutes.

6. Pour the red-cabbage juice into a bowl through a sieve (strain off all the cabbage and that, you get me?).

7. Wait for a while until the red-cabbage juice cools to room temperature.

8. Pour the red-cabbage juice into a drinking glass. After the experiment, you can save any leftover cabbage juice by putting it in a jar or Tupperware and keeping it in the fridge.

**Prepare acids and alkalis:**
1. Pour 50ml of vinegar into one glass.

2. Pour 50ml of lemon juice into another glass.

3. Pour 50ml of water into a glass and add two squirts of washing-up liquid, then mix.

4. Pour 50ml of water into the final glass.

**Test acids and alkalis:**
1. Pour two teaspoons of the red-cabbage juice into each glass.

2. See what colour each liquid turns.

3. Use the pH chart on the next page to find out the pH of the solution.

Now this is a special chart that is actually different from most pH charts, and it's designed to be used with a red-cabbage indicator. A regular pH chart would show strong acids as red and strong alkalis as purple — those are the colours that universal indicator paper will turn when it comes into contact with strong acids or alkalis. (Universal indicator paper is a strip of paper that is often used to test acids and alkalis in science labs.) But red-cabbage juice turns red for strong acids and yellow for strong alkalis, as we can see in the chart below.

| COLOUR | pH |
| --- | --- |
| Red | 2 |
| Pink | 4 |
| Purple | 6 |
| Violet | 7 |
| Blue | 8 |
| Green | 10 |
| Light Green | 12 |
| Yellow | 14 |

# RESULTS

So what happened when the red-cabbage juice was added to the different liquids? Lemon juice and vinegar are both acids, so they should have turned red or pink. Washing-up liquid, on the other hand, is an alkali, so it would have turned blue. Water is neither an acid nor an alkali, so it should have turned a nice violet colour.

# CONCLUSION

I guessed that lemon juice and vinegar were both acids, and my results show that I was right. What did you put down for soapy water and water? Was your hypothesis correct?

# EVALUATION

How could we make our experiment more accurate? Well, if you were doing this in a science lab you would use universal indicator paper, which is more accurate than red-cabbage juice.

## CHAPTER 6

## WHAT MAKES SOMETHING ACIDIC OR ALKALINE?

Let's take a closer look at these likkle acids and alkalis. We all know that lemons are sour, but why?

Lemons contain an acid called **CITRIC ACID**. Citric acid is what creates the sharp sourness that sizzles our mouth. Lemons aren't the only sour ones, though: oranges, grapefruits and pretty much all citrus fruits contain citric acid. However, most oranges don't have as much citric acid, so they're not as sour.

Vinegar is also acidic, but it contains a different type of acid called **ACETIC ACID**.

# I CAN'T ALKALIE

Alkalis such as washing-up liquid taste bitter because they contain a substance called sodium hydroxide. Sodium hydroxide is an alkali. **WAIT A MINUTE – SODIUM . . . WHERE HAVE WE HEARD THAT ELEMENT BEFORE?** From sodium chloride, also known as table salt!

Sodium is a metal that is present in both sodium chloride in salt and sodium hydroxide in washing-up liquid. In sodium hydroxide, the sodium bonds with oxygen and hydrogen instead of chlorine. Toothpaste also contains sodium hydroxide, which makes it an alkali. Many soaps and cleaners like laundry detergents also contain sodium hydroxide. This is the key ingredient that gets rid of dirt.

**DIFFICULTY LEVEL:** ⚡⚡⚡
Big Science

# EXPERIMENT 13: NEUTRALIZATION

### Ask a grown-up to help you with this one!

Ite cool — now that we know a bit more about acids and alkalis, we're going to do our own neutralization experiment. We're going to see if we can neutralize an acid with an alkali, using our leftover red-cabbage juice to test our mixture. What colour do you think the red-cabbage juice will turn when it's neutralized? Have a look back at the pH chart on p.134 and make your prediction.

Equipment list:
- ★ a pair of goggles
- ★ a measuring jug
- ★ two teaspoons of white distilled vinegar
- ★ two glasses
- ★ 90ml water
- ★ two teaspoons red-cabbage juice
- ★ washing-up liquid
- ★ a pipette
- ★ a spoon

## METHOD

1. Put your goggles on.

2. Measure out 10ml of vinegar in the measuring jug and pour it into one of the glasses.

3. Add 40ml of water to the vinegar to dilute it.

4. Add some red-cabbage juice to the diluted vinegar until it turns pink.

5. Put 8 squirts of washing-up liquid into the other glass and mix it in with 50ml of water.

6. Drop by drop, slowly add the soapy water to the vinegar, using the pipette.

7. Stir as you add the soapy water and watch as the solution changes colour.

8. When the solution turns violet, stop adding the soapy water.

## RESULTS

Our results show that the solution turned a nice violet colour — which means it has been neutralized! If you look at the pH chart, you'll see that a violet colour means pH 7, which is neutral. Neutralization is an example of an irreversible change.

## CONCLUSION

Did you predict the solution would turn violet? If so, nice one! How many drops of soapy water did it take to turn the solution neutral?

## EVALUATION

Is there anything you could have done differently in your experiment? Maybe you could have taken some photos of the mixture before and after the colour change? You could also repeat the experiment a few times to see if you need the same number of drops of soapy water each time. This would make your results more precise.

# I CAN'T ALKALIE

Do you know your acids and alkalis? Let's find out. Below we have a range of different acids and alkalis, and all you need to do is write which one is which. When you're finished, you can check your answers on p.200.

|  | ACID | ALKALI | NEUTRAL |
|---|---|---|---|
| Vinegar |  |  |  |
| Washing-up liquid |  |  |  |
| Water |  |  |  |
| Lemon juice |  |  |  |
| Grapefruit juice |  |  |  |
| Hydrochloric acid |  |  |  |
| Hand soap |  |  |  |
| Toothpaste |  |  |  |

# CHAPTER 6

## TRUE OR FALSE?

Are you ready to answer a few questions about acids and alkalis? I think you are. Here are six statements. Some of these statements are true, but some are false – can you work out which is which? When you're done, have a look at p.200 to make see if you got the right answers.

|  | TRUE | FALSE |
|---|---|---|
| A pH below 7 is acidic |  |  |
| Water is an acid |  |  |
| Washing-up liquid contains citric acid |  |  |
| Vinegar is an acid |  |  |
| A pH above 7 is an alkali |  |  |
| Washing-up liquid contains sodium hydroxide |  |  |

## I CAN'T ALKALIE

# WHEN ACIDS MEET ALKALIS

OK, so we know that when acids and alkalis are mixed together, they neutralize each other and that this is an irreversible change. Come on, you done know.

**LEVEL UP**

**But what else happens?**

We also know that in irreversible or chemical changes, a new product is created. So what else happens when you add an acid to an alkali? The neutralization reaction will always create a type of **SALT + WATER**. Salt doesn't always mean table salt that we sprinkle on food – there are lots of other chemical salts too.

We can write this reaction out as an equation and it would look something like this:

**Acid + Alkali ⟶ Salt + Water**

For example, mixing together hydrochloric acid (which is the acid in our stomachs) and sodium hydroxide would create sodium chloride – table salt! – plus water.

**Hydrochloric acid + Sodium hydroxide ⟶ Sodium chloride (salt) + Water**

> THINK ABOUT THOSE POPULAR KIDS AND THE LAID-BACK KIDS HAVING THAT FIGHT – SOMEONE IS GONNA END UP FEELING SALTY!

# CHAPTER 6

But what about those other types of salt that I mentioned? What do I even mean by 'salt'?

Well, in chemistry, we use salt to mean a type of substance that is produced in a neutralization reaction (although there are other ways to form salts too) and it usually has a particular structure. Remember the crystallization experiment and the little salt crystals we made? If you zoomed in on a different kind of salt – such as potassium chloride – it would have the same ordered, rigid structure that we saw in those crystals.

Potassium chloride a salt that is is made by the reaction of the alkali potassium hydroxide with hydrochloric acid. The equation for this reaction looks like this:

**Potassium hydroxide + Hydrochloric acid ⟶ Potassium chloride + Water**

There is also a special type of alkaline substance called a metal carbonate (such as sodium bicarbonate), which creates three products when reacted with acid – salt, water and carbon dioxide. We're about to test this in our next experiment!

**DIFFICULTY LEVEL:**
Come On Now

# EXPERIMENT 14: MAKING A LAVA LAMP

You can make your own lava lamp using a reaction between an acid and an alkali! You know those vitamin C tablets that fizz up when you put them into water? They contain an acid (citric acid) and an alkali (sodium bicarbonate).

When the tablet is put into water, the acid and alkali neutralize each other and release carbon dioxide gas. All of the fizzing and bubbles that we see is the carbon dioxide bubbling out of the water. The bubbles tell us that this is an irreversible or chemical change. So what do you think might happen when we add oil and food colouring into the mix? Write down your hypothesis!

Equipment list:
- ★ a pair of goggles
- ★ a glass
- ★ food colouring
- ★ 1/3 cup of water
- ★ 2/3 of a cup of cooking oil (such as sunflower or vegetable oil)
- ★ one vitamin C tablet

> This is another experiment that can sometimes leave a stain, so grab an old T-shirt or apron to wear and put down some newspaper or old tea towels on the work surface and floor, and ask an adult to help you.

## METHOD

1. Put your goggles on.

2. Fill up a quarter of a glass with water, then add twice as much oil to the water.

3. Next put in a couple of drops of food colouring of your choice.

4. Finally, we're going to drop the vitamin C tablet into the glass and watch the magic happen!

> YOU'LL NOTICE THAT THE WATER SINKS TO THE BOTTOM OF THE GLASS AND THE OIL FORMS A LAYER ON TOP - THIS IS BECAUSE WATER IS DENSER THAN OIL. HOW **DENSE** SOMETHING IS MEANS HOW TIGHTLY PACKED ITS PARTICLES ARE IN A GIVEN SPACE. THINGS THAT ARE DENSER THAN WATER WILL SINK, BUT THINGS THAT ARE LESS DENSE THAN WATER WILL FLOAT.

## RESULTS

What did we see when we added the vitamin C tablet to the glass? Bare bubbles and fizzing! The $CO_2$ was released as bubbles and travelled from the water at the bottom of the glass through the layer of oil. As the bubbles floated up and down, the food colouring swirled around, making it look like a colourful lava lamp. The $CO_2$ bubbles are less dense than both the water and the oil, which is why they rose to the top.

## CONCLUSION

Did you expect the bubbles to float to the top? And what did you think would happen to the food colouring and oil?

We can see that the oil and water do not mix because as we learned, the oil is less dense than the water. And the food colouring does not mix with the oil because it's soluble in water, but not oil. The food colouring turned the water a nice bright colour, and as the bubbles of carbon dioxide floated up to the top they pulled the colourful water droplets with them — creating awesome swirly patterns!

## EVALUATION

Could we have done anything differently? Yes — we could have used a measuring jug to measure out our oil and water. Done know.

**BOOM!** So we've met our cool acids and laid-back alkalis and figured out who's bare zesty and who's just bitter. So what are the key points we've learned from this chapter?

★ Acids have a pH between 0 and 6.

★ Alkalis have a pH between 8 and 14.

★ pH 7 is neutral.

★ pH indicators tell us the strength of the acid or alkali.

★ The lower the pH, the more acidic a liquid is.

★ The higher the pH, the more alkaline a liquid is.

★ An acid plus an alkali in equal parts make a neutralization reaction that results in a neutral pH of 7.

★ Acid plus alkali reactions make a salt plus water.

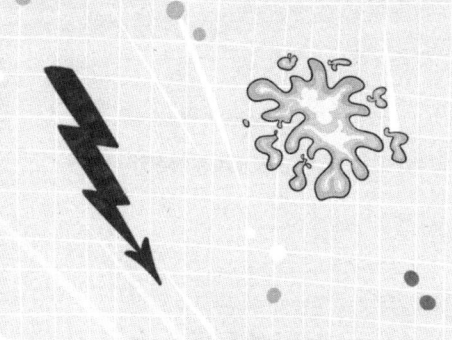

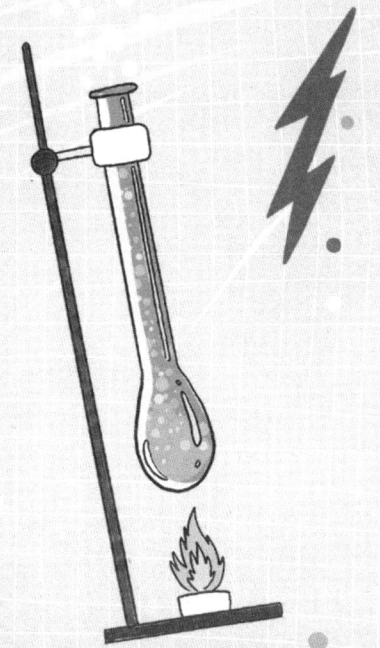

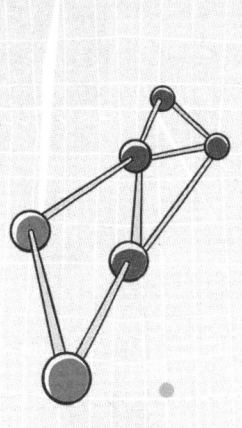

# CHAPTER 7
# BOOM!

## CHAPTER 7

OK, in this chapter we're gonna try out some cool experiments and chemical reactions that go **BOOM!**

We're also gonna look more closely at physical (reversible) and chemical (irreversible) changes. In each experiment, I want you to think about what type of reaction is taking place. Let's start off with a nice easy one.

**DIFFICULTY LEVEL:**
Simple Ting

# EXPERIMENT 15:
# CORNFLOUR + WATER

**BOOM!** We're going to mix some cornflour with water and see if the change is physical or chemical.

**Remember:** A chemical change always produces a new substance, but no new substances are made in a physical change.

If it's a physical change, then the cornflour may change into a different state. If it's a chemical change, we may see some fizzing or bubbling, or there could be a colour change or heat produced. What do you think will happen? Write down your hypothesis.

Equipment list:
- ★ one mug of cornflower
- ★ a bowl
- ★ half a mug of water

## METHOD

1. Pour one mug of cornflour into a bowl.

2. Mix half as much water into the cornflour and knead it with your hands.

3. As you knead it, the texture of the cornflour will change. How does it feel and look?

## RESULTS

You'll notice that it feels gel-like and squishy, almost like putty. The cornflour was a solid but when water was added, it changed into a different state!

## CONCLUSION

So — do you think this was a physical or a chemical change? If you said physical change — you're right! The gooey mixture is still made up of water and cornflour — they just look and feel different. We could separate out the water and cornflour by spreading the mixture on a flat surface and allowing the water to evaporate. This means this is a physical change and not a chemical one.

# EVALUATION

Is there anything we could have done to make our experiment more accurate? Yeah, we could have used a measuring jug instead of a mug to measure out our cornflour.

## IS IT A LIQUID? IS IT A SOLID?

Cornflour and water is a special and unique state of matter. It's not quite solid and it's not quite liquid – it's somewhere in between! This state is known as a **non-Newtonian fluid.** It can behave as both a liquid and a solid. If we dip our fingers into this mixture and move them around, it flows around just like a liquid. But if we give it a slap, it turns solid! When we apply pressure to a non-Newtonian fluid, the particles are compressed together and they can't slide over each other like in a liquid, so it becomes solid. When we remove the pressure, the particles are no longer compressed together and they can slide over each other, so it becomes a liquid. Mad tings!

**DIFFICULTY LEVEL:** ⚡⚡⚡
Big Science

# EXPERIMENT 16:
# VINEGAR + BAKING SODA

> **Ask a grown-up to help you with this one!**

Ite, BOOM! So right now we're going to do a LIT experiment. We're going to make a volcano! Obviously we're going to need some chemicals for this, init, so we're going to use some vinegar, which is an acid, and a bit of sodium bicarbonate, which is an alkali. Done know.

What we're going to do is mix them together and see what happens. If we see bare bubbles being produced, then that means an irreversible reaction has taken place. What do you think will happen when we add them together? Write down your hypothesis.

Equipment list:
- ★ a pair of goggles
- ★ newspaper or old tea towels
- ★ 200ml distilled white vinegar
- ★ a plastic bottle
- ★ a funnel
- ★ washing-up liquid
- ★ two heaped tablespoons sodium bicarbonate (baking soda)

## METHOD

1. Put your goggles on and pop down some newspaper or old tea towels where you're gonna do your experiment.

2. Pour the vinegar into the bottle using the funnel.

3. Then add two squirts of washing-up liquid into the bottle with the vinegar and swish it around.

4. This next step is the mad part. Make sure you've dried the funnel first, then take the two heaped tablespoons of sodium bicarbonate and pour it into the bottle using the funnel. What did you see happening when you mixed them together?

## RESULTS

There are bare bubbles and loads of fizzing because carbon dioxide gas is being released from the reaction. The vinegar reacts with the sodium bicarbonate to make **sodium acetate** (a type of salt), carbon dioxide and water. The washing-up liquid helps to trap the carbon dioxide gas and create lots of foam for our volcano!

## CONCLUSION

Reversible or irreversible? Was your hypothesis correct? Yes fam, it's irreversible because three products are made, and we wouldn't be able to turn them back into vinegar and sodium bicarbonate.

## EVALUATION

What else could we have done to make our experiment more accurate and precise? Can you think of anything?

> DID YOU KNOW THAT THIS REACTION IS ALSO AN EXAMPLE OF A NEUTRALIZATION REACTION? SODIUM BICARBONATE IS AN ALKALI AND VINEGAR IS AN ACID. NEUTRALIZATION REACTIONS ARE ALWAYS IRREVERSIBLE BECAUSE THEY CREATE NEW PRODUCTS, SALT AND WATER. DONE KNOW.

**DIFFICULTY LEVEL:**
Big Science

# EXPERIMENT 17:
# INFLATING A BALLOON

> **Ask a grown-up to help you with this one!**

Now we're going to do another reaction with vinegar and sodium bicarbonate, but this time we're going to use the carbon dioxide gas to inflate a balloon! Do you reckon this will be a reversible or irreversible reaction? Write down your hypothesis!

Equipment list:
- ★ a pair of goggles
- ★ 200ml distilled white vinegar
- ★ a funnel
- ★ three heaped tablespoons sodium bicarbonate (baking soda)
- ★ a balloon
- ★ a bottle

## METHOD

1. Put your goggles on.

2. Fill up a bottle with 200ml of vinegar using the funnel (just like before,) then dry the funnel.

3. Instead of putting the sodium bicarbonate straight into the vinegar, you're going to put it into a balloon. So put the end of the funnel into the top of the balloon and pour the sodium bicarbonate through the funnel into the balloon.

4. Remove the funnel then attach the top of the balloon to the top of the bottle. Let the bottom of the balloon hang down, so that the sodium bicarbonate doesn't go into the vinegar yet.

5. Once the balloon is securely fixed on to the bottle, lift up the bottom of the balloon to tip all of the sodium bicarbonate from the balloon into the vinegar and stand back.

6. As they react together, all of the carbon dioxide gas will be released and collected into the balloon. The balloon will inflate as the reaction takes place. Make sure you stand well back in case it pops!

## RESULTS

We can see that carbon dioxide gas has been released into our balloon. Just like before, three products have been made: sodium acetate, carbon dioxide and water.

## CONCLUSION

What did you predict would happen in this experiment? Was your hypothesis correct? Yes fam!

## EVALUATION

Is there anything you would have done differently? Which experiment worked better, the volcano or the balloon? Write down your observations.

_____

_____

_____

_____

_____

**DIFFICULTY LEVEL:** Big Science

# EXPERIMENT 18: TURNING MILK INTO PLASTIC

> **Ask a grown-up to help you with this one!**

I've got another mad experiment for us to do. We're going to turn milk into plastic! Do you think this will be a reversible or irreversible change? Write down your hypothesis.

Equipment list:
- ★ a pair of goggles
- ★ 150ml cow's milk
- ★ a saucepan
- ★ a hob
- ★ 15ml vinegar
- ★ a teaspoon
- ★ a piece of linen or cotton cloth
- ★ a glass
- ★ rubber band
- ★ a tissue

# METHOD

1. Put your goggles on.

2. Pour the milk into a saucepan.

3. Heat the milk on the hob until it begins to boil.

4. Remove the milk from the heat and add 15ml of vinegar to the saucepan.

5. Stir the mixture for a few minutes. It will separate out into a solid (curds) and liquid (whey).

6. Secure the cloth over the glass using a rubber band. Ensure that there's a dip in the middle of the cloth.

7. Pour the mixture through the cloth to separate the solid from the liquid.

8. Separate any remaining liquid from the solid by gathering the solid in the cloth and squeezing off as much liquid as possible.

9. Dry off the solid by patting it with a tissue.

10. Squash it all together and mould it into a pancake shape, then leave it to dry in a warm place for 48 hours.

11. You will be left with a brittle plastic.

## RESULTS

After the solid has dried, write down a description of what it looks and feels like. Now that you can see the results, what type of reaction do you think this is?

## CONCLUSION

If you said irreversible — you're right! We can't turn the plastic back into milk, so this is a chemical change.

**But why does this reaction create plastic?**
Milk contains a **protein** called casein. Casein molecules are curled up into themselves like a ball. When you add vinegar to the milk, the casein molecules unfold themselves and form long chains. The long chains then

### CASEIN
Casein is also the name of a natural type of plastic that was used in the 1900s to make buttons, pens, combs, brushes and mirrors.

hook on to each other and form plastic. Plastics are always made up of molecules in these long chains.

## EVALUATION

Did the experiment work as expected? What type of cloth did you use? Write down anything you noticed.

_____
_____
_____
_____
_____
_____
_____
_____
_____
_____

**DIFFICULTY LEVEL:**
Big Science

# EXPERIMENT 19:
# ELEPHANT'S TOOTHPASTE

> **Ask a grown-up to help you with this one!**

For our next **BIG SCIENCE** experiment we're going to try making 'elephant's toothpaste'! This is a fun experiment that makes a crazy foam explosion. Reversible or irreversible — what do you predict?

> You can try this one at home but only with an adult to help you as we're using hydrogen peroxide, which can be harmful if it gets on your skin. Make sure you put down some newspaper or old tea towels to protect surfaces and the floor, and that you're wearing old clothes, as the mixture could stain!

Equipment list:
- ★ a pair of goggles
- ★ food colouring
- ★ two glasses
- ★ 75ml warm water
- ★ a teaspoon
- ★ a pair of rubber gloves (you and your adult need to wear these when handling chemicals)
- ★ 75ml of 3% hydrogen peroxide solution (available to buy from pharmacies)
- ★ two teaspoons of washing-up liquid
- ★ four sachets of dry powdered yeast (available to buy in large supermarkets)

## METHOD

1. Put on your gloves and goggles.

2. Fill the glass with 75ml of 3% hydrogen peroxide solution and add two teaspoons of washing-up liquid.

3. Then add a few drops of food colouring as well.

4. Pour four sachets of powdered yeast into a separate glass and add 75ml of warm water. Mix them well with a teaspoon.

5. Add your yeast mixture to the hydrogen peroxide in the glass and stand back. This will make the hydrogen peroxide shoot out loads of foam!

6. Once the foam has cooled, keep your gloves on and get an adult to help you dispose of the foam safely in the bin.

## RESULTS

The yeast causes the hydrogen peroxide to break down and release large amounts of oxygen. All of the foam being released is bubbles of oxygen, and the food colouring turned the foam a cool colour!

## CONCLUSION

Was your prediction correct? If you said irreversible, you're right, fam — we know this is an irreversible reaction because of all the gas being produced. And did you notice that the foam feels warm? This is because the reaction is **exothermic**, which means it releases heat!

## EVALUATION

If you wanted to be *really* precise with your measurements, you could have tested the temperature of the mixture using a thermometer before you added the yeast, and then tested it again afterwards. The change in temperature shows that an exothermic reaction has taken place. Find out more on the next page!

BOOM!

# EXOTHERMIC AND ENDOTHERMIC REACTIONS

LEVEL UP

An exothermic reaction is a reaction that releases heat. Combustion reactions are great examples of exothermic reactions because they release large amounts of heat energy.

Neutralization reactions between an acid and an alkali are nearly always exothermic too. The solution feels hotter when they react together, which means that heat energy is released.

The opposite of an exothermic reaction is an **endothermic** one. These reactions actually feel colder. Citric acid from lemon juice plus sodium bicarbonate is an endothermic reaction – this means the solution gets colder when you mix the two ingredients, as the solution absorbs heat energy.

If you want to find out whether a reaction is exothermic or endothermic, all you need to do is measure the temperature of the substances before and after the reaction. If the temperature increases after the reaction, then it's exothermic. If the temperature decreases after the reaction, then it's endothermic.

**BOOM!** We've done some mad experiments in this chapter and learned a bit more about reversible and irreversible changes, plus endothermic and exothermic reactions – big science tings.

I think you're getting pretty good at this now, so instead of giving you the key points, I'm gonna test your knowledge of reversible and irreversible changes, based on what you learned in this chapter and earlier in the book. Find the answers on p.200.

|  | TRUE | FALSE |
|---|---|---|
| Melting ice is a reversible change |  |  |
| Baking a cake is a reversible change |  |  |
| An irreversible change is one that can be changed back |  |  |
| An exothermic reaction releases heat |  |  |
| Reversible changes don't create new materials |  |  |
| An endothermic reaction will feel warm |  |  |
| Burning a candle is a reversible change |  |  |
| Combustion is an exothermic reaction |  |  |

# CHAPTER 8
# EVEN BIGGER SCIENCE

**CHAPTER 8**

# EVEN BIGGER SCIENCE

**LEVEL UP**

In this book, we've looked at **SIMPLE TING** experiments right the way up to **BIG SCIENCE** experiments. But this is just the beginning! There's loads more mad experiments you can do when you get older. In this chapter, I'm gonna give you a little taste of some of them. All of the experiments I talk about in this chapter are proper advanced science that you can only do in a lab with supervision from a teacher, so DON'T try these at home. (Apart from p .179–182 – this is a big science experiment that you can actually do yourself with help from an adult!)

## MAD METALS

The longer you study it, the more exciting science gets. If you choose to study science at secondary school or even at university, you'll get the opportunity to experiment with all of the different elements that exist. Some of my favourite elements are alkali metals – these things are mad reactive!

Alkali metals are not hard and tough like **IRON**, for example. These metals are bare soft and squishy. They're so soft that you can actually cut them with a knife like butter. Imagine a soft metal that you could

## EVEN BIGGER SCIENCE

literally squash between your fingers. That's crazy! Some examples of alkali metals are **SODIUM**, **LITHIUM** and **POTASSIUM**. Remember how I said at the start of the book that you don't want to mess with sodium? Well – I'm about to tell you why!

If a small piece of sodium metal is put into a bowl of water, the sodium would set on fire. The flaming fireball of sodium would then skate along the surface of the water and fizz like mad.

After a few seconds, we would hear a massive BANG as the sodium fireball would explode in all directions, shooting out yellow fire and melted sodium metal. Mad ting!

## CHAPTER 8

**LEVEL UP**

Potassium metal makes an even bigger explosion when it's put into water, and it creates purple flames as it explodes. Lithium is the least reactive out of the alkali metals and makes the smallest explosion, but it does produce some nice red flames.

Because these alkali metals are so mad reactive, we can't just leave them out on the table – they might catch fire! That's because they'll react with the oxygen and water in the air and start burning. We have to store them inside containers of oil so that no air or water can get to them and cause a reaction.

**Caesium** and **rubidium** metals are even crazier and more reactive than sodium and potassium. They're so reactive that as soon as they're exposed to air, they will melt into a liquid and explode! Caesium and rubidium can't even be stored in oil – they have to be kept in a container with a gas called argon. **Argon** gas is unreactive, so the metals won't explode.

> BOOM! ALKALI METALS ARE MAD COOL – MAYBE YOU'VE SEEN ME DOING EXPERIMENTS WITH THEM ONLINE?

# EVEN BIGGER SCIENCE

## COLOURED FLAMES

There are also special salts that can produce bare colourful flames – just like the colours you see in fireworks!

As we know from learning about salts earlier in the book, there are lots of different chemical salts that contain different metals. Sodium chloride (table salt) contains sodium. Lithium chloride contains – you guessed it – lithium! Sodium chloride produces a yellow flame when you burn it, and lithium chloride produces a red flame. Here are some of the other salts and their crazy coloured flames:

| | |
|---|---|
| **Copper chloride** | Green flame |
| **Potassium chloride** | Purple flame |
| **Calcium chloride** | Orange flame |
| **Lithium chloride** | Red flame |
| **Sodium chloride** | Yellow flame |
| **Barium chloride** | Green flame |
| **Iron chloride** | Yellow flame |

## CHAPTER 8

**LEVEL UP**

To create some coloured flames in your school science lab, your teacher or science technician would use a pair of tongs to hold the salt over the flame from a Bunsen burner (making sure they were wearing goggles!). Then you'd see the salt catch alight with a beautiful bright colour!

### BUNSEN BURNER

A Bunsen burner is a special device used for heating things in experiments. It's made of a metal cylinder attached to a rubber tube, which is connected to a gas tap that has methane gas flowing through it. When you hold a match above it, the gas lights to produce a hot flame. There's a small air hole at the bottom of the Bunsen that can be opened to let more oxygen in. When the hole is open, the flame turns blue and makes a loud noise. This blue flame is called a roaring flame and is much hotter than the yellow flame produced when the air hole is closed.

# EVEN BIGGER SCIENCE

## POP, BUBBLE AND SQUEAK

Ite cool, so earlier in the book we met our friends hydrogen and oxygen. And you know how oxygen likes to get lit – well, hydrogen likes to get fully **EXPLOSIVE!** Pure hydrogen gas is one of the most explosive gases in the world. If a flame is put anywhere near hydrogen gas, it will instantly explode and create bare hot flames. So remember, this test is **NOT** one you can try at home – but a chemistry teacher can show you in a lab.

> STAND BACK – iT'S GONNA BE A MAD TiNG.

Let's say you've just done an experiment where hydrogen gas is produced. You can't see the hydrogen, so how do you know it's there?

## CHAPTER 8

**LEVEL UP**

You would do what we scientists call the squeaky pop test. First, you would hold your thumb over the test tube to stop the hydrogen gas from coming out. Then you would remove your thumb and hold a lit match close to the test tube. If you hear a squeaky pop sound when you put the flame inside the test tube, that means you've made hydrogen gas! That squeaky pop sound is actually a mini explosion created by igniting the hydrogen gas in the test tube.

There's a test that you can do for oxygen gas too. First, you would light a match and then blow it out so that's it's still glowing at the end. If you hold the glowing match next to a test tube filled with oxygen, the match will magically relight! This is because – as we know – oxygen is needed for things to burn, and with enough oxygen you can turn even a tiny bit of heat into a flame!

And what if you wanted to test for carbon dioxide? Remember the carbon dioxide bubbles we made when we reacted vinegar with baking soda? If we were to trap that gas in a container and then add a solution called lime water, which is made from calcium hydroxide and water, we could find out if it really is carbon dioxide. Lime water is a clear and transparent liquid (just like regular water), but it turns to a milky white colour when you pass carbon dioxide through it. That's because the calcium hydroxide solution reacts with the carbon dioxide to produce something called calcium carbonate, which has a milky white colour. Mad tings!

## METHANE BUBBLES

This next experiment is a mad ting: it involves creating flames from your bare hands! This sounds crazy but trust me – it doesn't hurt. Again, this is **NOT** one you can try at home – this is defo only to be tried in a science lab with supervision from your teacher.

## CHAPTER 8

**LEVEL UP**

In your school science lab, you would get a big bowl and fill it up with soapy water.

Then your teacher would attach one end of a rubber tube to a gas tap (this is a special tap you get in a science lab that turns on to release gas), with the other end in the soapy water. They'd turn on the tap to allow a stream of gas to flow into the water. This will make loads of big methane bubbles on the surface of the water.

Next, you would wet your hands and scoop up a big pile of bubbles.

Then you would hold your hands right out away from your body as the teacher uses a match to light the methane bubbles. You would end up with a massive flame coming out of your hands!

The flame won't hurt you, though, because your hands are wet. The layer of water protects your hands from the heat so they don't burn. But it looks like you're making fire from your hands!

**DIFFICULTY LEVEL:**
Big Science

# EXPERIMENT 20: EXTRACTING DNA

> **Ask a grown-up to help you with this one!**

Those are some of my favourite experiments that you might get to try in your secondary-school science lab. But I wanna leave you with one final BIG SCIENCE experiment that you can actually try at home.

This experiment allows you to extract DNA from a piece of fruit! But what is DNA?

> DNA stands for deoxyribonucleic acid (WOAH, that's a mad word!), and is a material found inside all living cells that tells the organism how to grow. It's like a kind of instruction manual for your cells, and it controls things such as your hair colour, eye colour and height. Even fruits like bananas and strawberries contain DNA that controls how they grow, their colour and how sweet they are.

Ite cool, man's gonna tell you how to extract the DNA from a strawberry. Any guesses on how the DNA might look? Write down your hypothesis!

---

Equipment list:
- ★ a pair of goggles
- ★ rubber gloves
- ★ a strawberry
- ★ a ziplock plastic bag
- ★ 30ml water
- ★ two teaspoons of washing-up liquid
- ★ one teaspoon of salt
- ★ a teaspoon of rubbing alcohol (isopropanol alcohol)
- ★ a spoon

---

## METHOD

1. Put on your goggles and your gloves.

2. Then put the strawberry into the sealed plastic bag and squash it until it becomes all mushy. This breaks up the cell walls of the strawberry.

3. Then you add in a mixture of soapy water and salt to the crushed-up strawberry. This mixture is prepared by mixing 30ml of water with one teaspoon of salt and two teaspoons of washing-up liquid. The soapy

water and salt will dissolve the **cell membrane** (which is like the wall of the cell) of the strawberry's cells and all of the DNA will be released.

4. Next, we need to separate the DNA from all of the mushy strawberry using the rubbing alcohol. When you add the alcohol, all of the DNA will float to the top! It looks like white stringy threads that stick together, and they can be scooped out with a spoon.

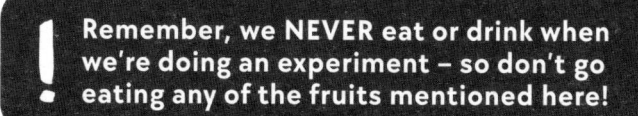

> ! Remember, we NEVER eat or drink when we're doing an experiment – so don't go eating any of the fruits mentioned here!

## RESULTS

Big tings! We successfully extracted our strawberry DNA. The alcohol works to separate out the DNA because DNA is not soluble in alcohol, so it clumps together and becomes visible.

## CONCLUSION

Was your hypothesis correct? Did the DNA look like you expected?

## EVALUATION

Is there anything we could have done differently in our experiment? Well, we could repeat this a few times with different strawberries to see if we get the same result — that would make our results more precise. You could try this experiment with kiwis, pineapples and bananas too!

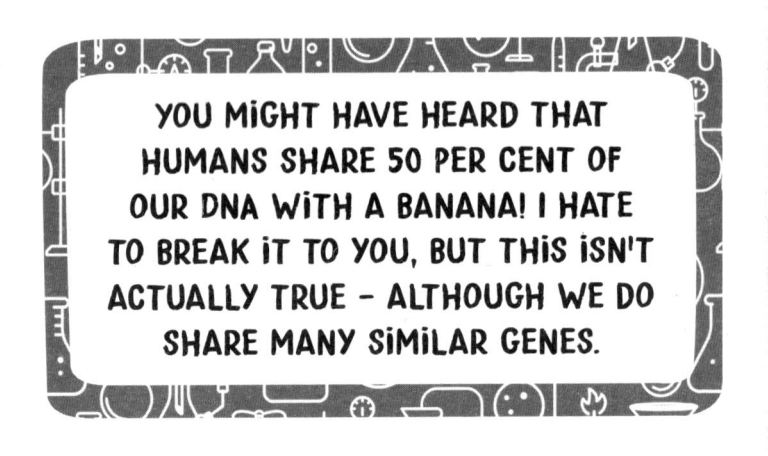

> **YOU MIGHT HAVE HEARD THAT HUMANS SHARE 50 PER CENT OF OUR DNA WITH A BANANA! I HATE TO BREAK IT TO YOU, BUT THIS ISN'T ACTUALLY TRUE - ALTHOUGH WE DO SHARE MANY SIMILAR GENES.**

# SCIENCE LESSON COMPLETED (CONCLUSION)

## CONCLUSION

**BOOM!** Well done for getting to the end of the book – man's a proper scientist now!

We met some cool characters like oxygen, sodium, chlorine, hydrogen and carbon. We found out about their personalities and why some of them are besties and some aren't. Like, sodium gets on with everyone because it's really reactive! But carbon loves bonding with hydrogen to make hydrocarbons, or fuels.

We also learned that oxygen loves to get lit! It's the main character when it comes to combustion. If there's a fire, you can guarantee oxygen will be there, along with a fuel and heat.

We met those zesty acids and bitter alkalis, and the kid who's always in the middle – $H_2O$. How did we find out how zesty or bitter these acids and alkalis are? The pH scale! Whenever those acids come across the alkalis, they always neutralize each other and the pH becomes a neutral 7.

Remember the chemical couples that we learned about too? Hydrogen and oxygen are a couple,

## SCIENCE LESSON COMPLETED

along with sodium and chlorine. Sometimes they mix things up and hang out with each other, but they always return to their couples.

And what about the different moods that we see our characters go through – a.k.a. the states of matter? We know that when particles get more energy they go from sleepy (solid) to awake (liquid), and even more energy gets them excited and turns them into a gas!

Through meeting all these cool and crazy elements, we've discovered how they react to each other and what to expect from our experiments. And that's what chemistry is all about – looking at how matter behaves, making predictions and testing them out. Done know. Chemistry tings.

## CONCLUSION

You might remember at the start of the book I said that science is all about asking questions. And this is the message I want to leave you with:

### CURIOSITY IS THE KEY TO BEING A GREAT SCIENTIST.

If you encounter something that you don't understand, then ask questions to try to figure it out. Science is about looking deeper into things and trying to understand how and why something works. If you don't ask, then you'll never know. Sometimes we can be a bit afraid to ask questions because we're worried that other people might laugh at us for not knowing – but asking questions is the best thing that you can do because it will expand your knowledge! Always be curious. Curiosity will give you the answers that you're looking for.

*BIG MANNY*

## WHICH ELEMENT ARE YOU?

Now that you've met the elements in the book, perhaps you're wondering which type of element YOU would be? Answer the questions below to find out!

1. **Are you . . .**
**A** making new friends all the time
**B** someone who brings people together
**C** the life of the party
**D** someone who prefers hanging out with just one person

2. **In the summer, do you . . .**
**A** avoid the beach because you hate getting wet
**B** love jumping in the pool
**C** enjoy being in the sun
**D** love a big barbecue

3. **Are you . . .**
**A** a big softie
**B** a peacemaker
**C** someone who gets into heated arguments
**D** often described as tough

**ANSWERS:**

**If you answered mostly A, you are sodium!**
Sodium HATES getting wet (remember, it explodes in water), but is good at making friends (cos its very reactive) – and they are really a big softie (because it's soft and squishy at room temperature!).

**If you answered mostly B, you are chlorine!**
Chlorine absolutely loves swimming (it keeps swimming pools clean), and it's always a pleasure to be around because it gets on with everyone (chlorine is very reactive – so can form bonds with lots of different elements!)

**If you answered mostly C, you are oxygen!**
Oxygen is fiery and can light up almost anything. It's the centre of attention and everyone needs a bit of oxygen in their life. Where would we be without it?!

**If you answered mostly D, you are carbon!**
Carbon is quite a tough cookie and can often be found by itself (as charcoal!). It's full of energy and loves summer BBQs. If it's not alone, carbon can often be found hanging out with just one other element, like hydrogen or oxygen.

## BIG MANNY'S BIG QUIZ!

OK – it's time to test if you've been paying attention with my BIG QUIZ. Have a go at the questions below (no cheating!).

1. **What is a hypothesis?**
**A** A hypothesis is how you're going to do the experiment.
**B** A hypothesis is what you think the outcome of the experiment will be.

2. **In which section of your scientific write-up do you say whether your hypothesis was correct or not?**
**A** Method
**B** Conclusion
**C** Evaluation

3. **How do you make an experiment more precise?**
**A** Repeat the experiment
**B** Use more variables

4. Can you work out which of the below statements are true or false?

i. You have more control over variables in a fair test.
A True
B False

ii. A correlation means a relationship between two variables.
A True
B False

iii. Elements are made up of just one type of atom
A True
B False

iv. The particles in a solid are packed together more tightly than in a liquid.
A True
B False

v. The particles in a gas are packed together very tightly.
A True
B False

5. **What makes the particles in a solid pack together tightly?**
   A   Forces of attraction
   B   Heat

6. **Which state of matter can be compressed (squashed) into a smaller space?**
   A   Solid
   B   Liquid
   C   Gas

7. **What is the process of turning a solid into a liquid?**
   A   Boiling
   B   Melting
   C   Evaporating
   D   Condensing

8. **Which state of matter can be held in your hand?**
   A   Solid
   B   Liquid
   C   Gas

YOU GOT THIS, FAM!

9. **Which state of matter can be poured?**
A  Solid
B  Liquid
C  Gas

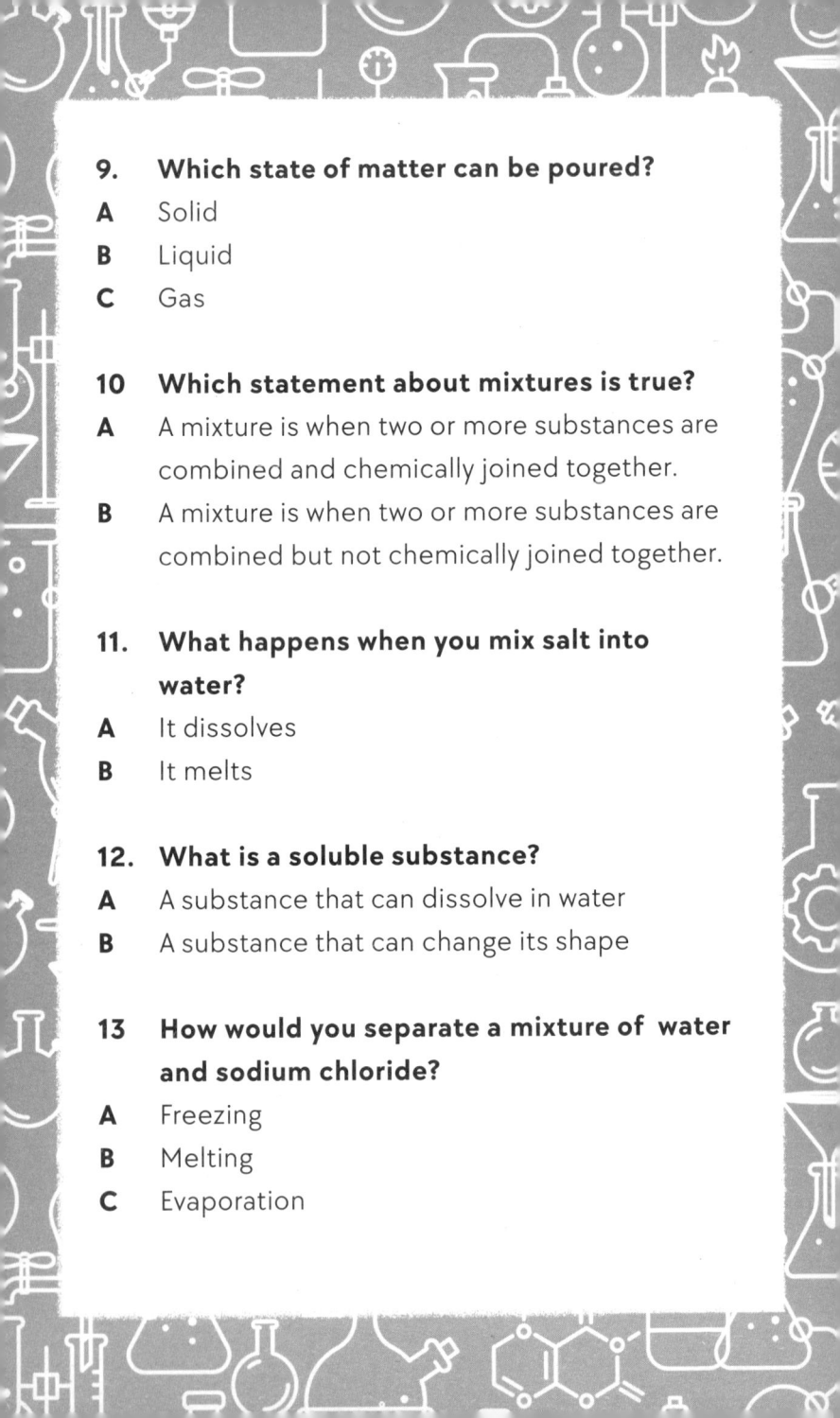

10 **Which statement about mixtures is true?**
A  A mixture is when two or more substances are combined and chemically joined together.
B  A mixture is when two or more substances are combined but not chemically joined together.

11. **What happens when you mix salt into water?**
A  It dissolves
B  It melts

12. **What is a soluble substance?**
A  A substance that can dissolve in water
B  A substance that can change its shape

13 **How would you separate a mixture of water and sodium chloride?**
A  Freezing
B  Melting
C  Evaporation

**14. Which of these mixtures can be separated by sieving?**

**A** Salt and water

**B** Oil and water

**C** Sand and stones

**15. Which solvent do you use to separate the pigments in ink?**

**A** Water

**B** Oil

**16. What happens during distillation?**

**A** A liquid is heated into a gas and then condensed back into a liquid.

**B** A liquid is frozen into a solid and then melted again.

**17. What is boiling point?**

**A** The temperature at which a solid turns into a liquid.

**B** The temperature at which a liquid turns into a gas.

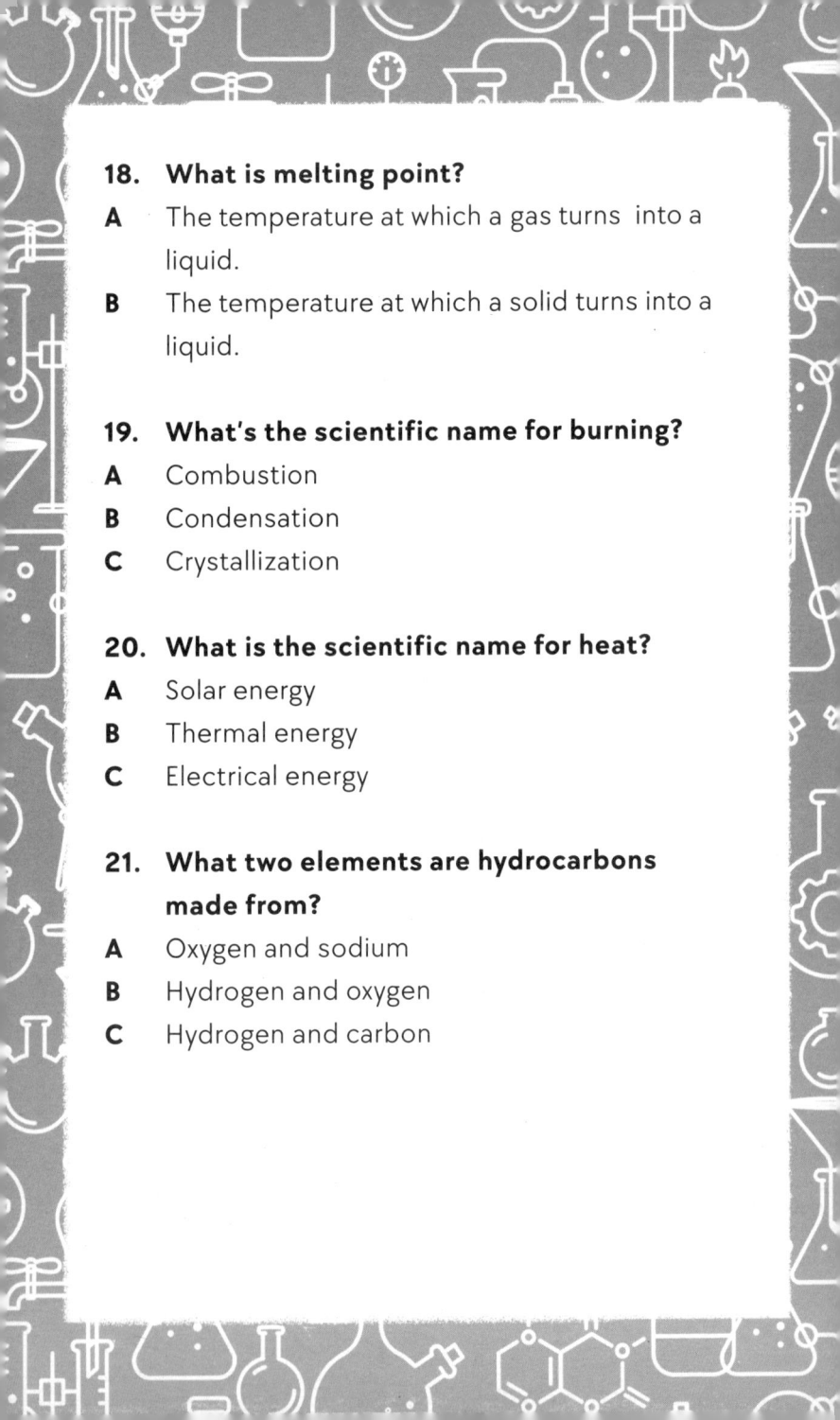

**18. What is melting point?**
A   The temperature at which a gas turns into a liquid.
B   The temperature at which a solid turns into a liquid.

**19. What's the scientific name for burning?**
A   Combustion
B   Condensation
C   Crystallization

**20. What is the scientific name for heat?**
A   Solar energy
B   Thermal energy
C   Electrical energy

**21. What two elements are hydrocarbons made from?**
A   Oxygen and sodium
B   Hydrogen and oxygen
C   Hydrogen and carbon

**22. Complete the sentences below using the words in bold.**

**A** When a _____ is burned, it is _____ by the oxygen in the air. This process is known as _____.

**(fuel, combustion, oxidized)**

**B** When a _____ is burned, the products made are _____ and _____.

**(carbon dioxide, fuel, water)**

**C** An irreversible change is a change that _____ be undone. A reversible change is a change that _____ be undone.

**(can, can't)**

**23. Which change is reversible?**

**A** Burning wood
**B** Freezing water
**C** Mixing cement

**24. Which change is irreversible?**

**A** Evaporation
**B** Boiling
**C** Frying an egg

**25.** **Complete the sentences below using the words in bold.**

(HINT: you won't need to use all of the words)

**A** In a _____ reaction, no new products are made. In an _____ reaction, new products are made.

**(irreversible, reversible, edible)**

**B** If we remove _____ from a fire, the fire will be _____.

**(oxygen, helium, extinguished, bigger)**

**C** The products made from _____ combustion are _____ carbon dioxide and water.

**(incomplete, complete, carbon monoxide)**

**26. Select the acid.**

**A** Water
**B** Washing-up liquid
**C** Lemon juice

**27. Select the alkali.**

**A** Washing-up liquid
**B** Vinegar
**C** Water

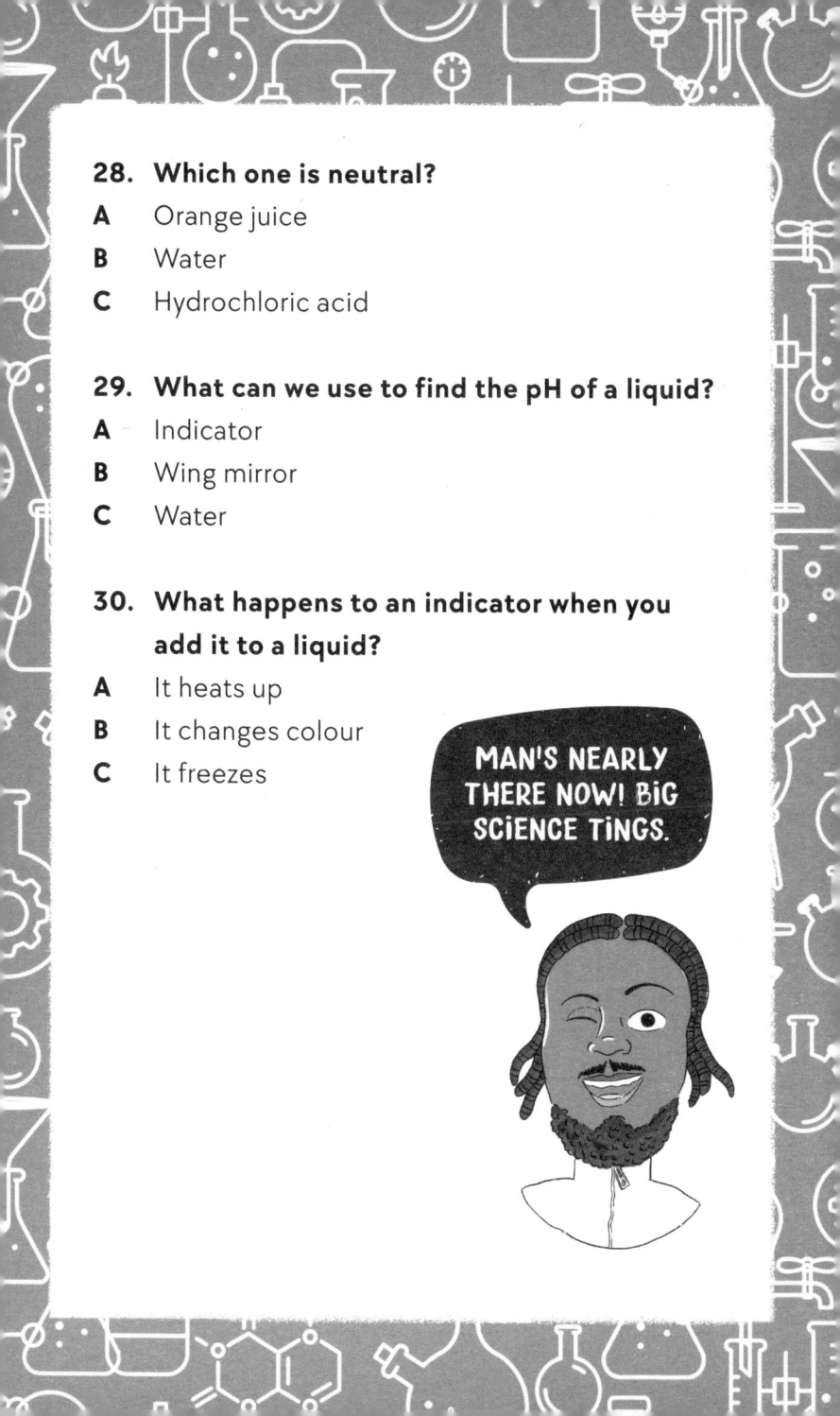

### 28. Which one is neutral?
**A** Orange juice
**B** Water
**C** Hydrochloric acid

### 29. What can we use to find the pH of a liquid?
**A** Indicator
**B** Wing mirror
**C** Water

### 30. What happens to an indicator when you add it to a liquid?
**A** It heats up
**B** It changes colour
**C** It freezes

MAN'S NEARLY THERE NOW! BiG SCiENCE TiNGS.

**ANSWERS TO PAGES 31-32:**

**2. Comparative test.** We are comparing the two cars here to see which one goes further, but there are many things we can't control – such as the material the cars are made from and how heavy they are – which could affect our results.

**3. Fair test.** We are only changing one variable: the supply of oxygen to the candle.

**4. Comparative test.** We are comparing different tissues in this test. There are other variables such as the thickness of the tissue and the type of material it's made from, which we can't control.

**5. Comparative test.** We are comparing different materials, but we don't know exactly why some may be more reflective than others – it could be to do with the colour or smoothness, for example. So there are some variables beyond our control.

**ANSWERS TO PAGES 37-38:**

**Hypothesis:** I think that the toy car will travel further on the wooden floor than the carpet when pushed with equal force.

**Independent variable:** The floor type

**Dependent variable:** Distance travelled by the toy car

**Control:** Car we are using

**Conclusion:** The car travelled further on the wooden floor so my prediction was correct. This experiment is a fair test as we are only changing one variable – the floor type (as long as other variables such as the force used to push the car are kept the same).

**ANSWERS TO PAGE 46:**

Jelly – Solid
Ice cream – Solid
Butter – Solid
Olive oil – Liquid
Rice – Solid
Syrup – Liquid
Salt – Solid
Wood – Solid
Plastic – Solid
Steam – Gas
Carbon Dioxide – Gas
Sand – Solid
Water – Liquid

**ANSWERS TO PAGE 52:**

| Solid | → | **Liquid** – melting |
| Liquid | → | **Solid** – freezing |
| Gas | → | **Liquid** – condensing |
| Liquid | → | **Gas** – evaporating or boiling |

## ANSWERS TO PAGE 81:

Rice and oil: filtrate = oil, residue = rice
Water and soil: filtrate = water, residue = soil
Cereal and milk: filtrate = milk, residue = cereal

## ANSWERS TO PAGES 141:

Vinegar – Acid
Washing-up liquid – Alkali
Water – Neutral
Lemon juice – Acid
Grapefruit juice – Acid
Hydrochloric acid – Acid
Hand soap – Alkali
Toothpaste – Alkali

## ANSWERS TO PAGE 142:

A pH below 7 is acidic: TRUE
Water is an acid: FALSE
Washing-up liquid contains citric acid: FALSE
Vinegar is an acid: TRUE
A pH above 7 is an alkali: TRUE
Washing-up liquid contains sodium hydroxide: TRUE

## ANSWERS TO PAGE 168:

Melting ice is a reversible change: TRUE
Baking a cake is a reversible change: FALSE
An irreversible change is one that can be changed back: FALSE
An exothermic reaction releases heat: TRUE
Reversible changes don't create new materials: TRUE
An endothermic reaction will feel warm: FALSE
Burning a candle is a reversible change: FALSE
Combustion is an exothermic reaction: TRUE

## ANSWERS TO PAGES 189-199:

**1.** B
**2.** B
**3.** A
**4.** **I.** A
　　**II.** A
　　**III.** A
　　**IV.** A
　　**V.** B
**5.** A
**6.** C
**7.** B
**8.** A
**9.** B
**10.** A
**11.** A
**12.** A
**13.** C
**14.** C
**15.** A
**16.** A
**17.** B
**18.** B
**19.** A
**20.** B
**21.** C
**22.** **A** fuel, oxidized, combustion
　　**B** fuel, carbon dioxide, water
　　**C** can't, can,
**23.** B
**24.** C
**25.** **A** reversible, irreversible
　　**B** oxygen, extinguished,
　　**C** incomplete, carbon, monoxide
**26.** C
**27.** A
**28.** B
**29.** A
**30.** B

# GLOSSARY

**Accuracy** – a measurement of how close a result is to the correct result.

**Acetic acid** – a colourless acid that gives vinegar its characteristic smell and taste.

**Acid** – a substance with a pH value between 0 and 7.

**Alkali** – a substance with a pH value between 7 and 14.

**Argon** – an unreactive, colourless, odourless gas of the noble gas group (a group of gases which exist as single atoms and are unreactive).

**Atom** – the building blocks of matter. At the centre of the atom is a nucleus made up of particles called neutrons and protons. The atom also contains electrons, which travel around the nucleus. Different elements have different numbers of neutrons, protons and electrons. Electrons have a negative charge, protons have a positive charge and neutrons have no charge.

**Boiling** – the process of turning a liquid into a gas by rapid heating.

**Boiling point** – the temperature at which a liquid turns into a gas.

# GLOSSARY

**Butane** – a flammable hydrocarbon gas made from petroleum and natural gas. It's used in bottled form
as a fuel.

**Caesium** – a soft, silvery, extremely reactive alkali metal.

**Carbon dioxide** – a colourless and odourless gas that is produced in combustion, and also when humans breathe out!

**Carbon monoxide** – a colourless, odourless, flammable and toxic gas formed from the incomplete combustion
of fuels.

**Casein** – the main protein found in milk and cheese.

**Cell** – the smallest form of life that makes up larger organisms. Cells contain the DNA and proteins that allow plants and animals to grow.

**Cell membrane** – a thin layer that surrounds the cell like a coat. It controls what enters and exits the cell and separates the inside of the cell from the outside environment.

# GLOSSARY

**Celsius** – a scale of temperature on which water freezes at 0 degrees, and boils at 100 degrees, under standard conditions.

**Chemical equation** – the reactants and products in a chemical reaction represented by the chemical formula of the elements and molecules.

**Chromatography** – separating components of a mixture by passing it through a solvent.

**Combustion** – the process of burning something.

**Complete combustion** – when a hydrocarbon fuel has a good supply of air and all of the carbon and hydrogen atoms in the hydrocarbon react with oxygen in the air to produce carbon dioxide and water. Energy is also released in the form of heat and light.

**Compress** – to press or squeeze something together to reduce its size and volume.

**Conclusion** – a summary of the results and statement of whether the hypothesis was true or false.

**Condensation** – the process of cooling down a gas into a liquid.

# GLOSSARY

**Controls** – things in the experiment that we keep the same.

**Controlled environment** – a space where environmental factors such as temperature, pressure, light and air-flow are regulated and kept at the same level. This improves the reliability and accuracy of the experiment.

**Correlation** – the relationship between two variables.

**Crystallization** – the process of solids forming into an organized structure known as a crystal.

**Data** – information such as facts and numbers used to analyse something or make a conclusion.

**Dense** – where particles are tightly packed in a given space.

**Dependent variable** – the variable that is being measured during the experiment.

**Diffuse** – the movement of a liquid or gas from an area where particles are densely packed to one where they are less densely packed.

# GLOSSARY

**Directly proportional** – related, so that when one becomes larger or smaller, the other also becomes larger or smaller at the same rate.

**Dissolve** – when a soluble solid is mixed into a liquid and is incorporated into it.

**Distillation** – the process of purifying a liquid by boiling it into a gas and condensing it back into a liquid.

**Electrostatic force** – a force of attraction between atoms.

**Element** – substance made from only one sort of atom.

**Endothermic** – a type of reaction that takes in energy from the surroundings, so the reaction mixture feels cooler.

**Ethane** – a colourless, odourless, flammable gas derived from petroleum and natural gas. It's involved in the production of plastics.

**Evaluation** – a statement of how the experiment could be improved in terms of accuracy and precision.

## GLOSSARY

**Evaporation** – the process of gradually heating a liquid into a gas.

**Exothermic** – a type of reaction that releases heat.

**Expand** – when a substance increases in size.

**Extinguish** – cause a fire to stop burning.

**Filtrate** – a liquid which has passed through a filter.

**Filtration** – the process of passing a mixture of a solid and a liquid through a filter to remove the solid.

**Formula** – a set of symbols showing what a chemical compound (a substance made from more than one element bonded together) is made up of.

**Fractional distillation** – the process of separating a liquid mixture into different components according to their different boiling points.

**Freeze** – the process of cooling a liquid into a solid.

**Freezing point** – the temperature at which a liquid cools into a solid.

# GLOSSARY

**Fuel** – a material such as coal, gas or oil that is burned to produce heat or power.

**Gas** – a state of matter in which the particles are spread out from each other and can move around easily. Gases can be compressed and can change their shape.

**Helium** – an unreactive, colourless, odourless gas.

**Hydrocarbons** – substances made from hydrogen and carbon atoms.

**Hydrochloric acid** – a strongly acidic solution produced by dissolving of hydrogen chloride gas into water. Also found naturally in our stomachs.

**Hypothesis** – a statement of what you think the outcome of the experiment will be.

**Incomplete combustion** – the process of burning a fuel without enough oxygen, which results in the production of carbon monoxide, water and particulate carbon (or soot).

**Independent variable** – the variable that is changed during the experiment.

**Inorganic** – not made from natural materials.

# GLOSSARY

**Insoluble** – a substance that is unable to dissolve into a solvent.

**Invalid** – when the results of an experiment are not right because of incorrect information or because they can't be repeated.

**Irreversible change/chemical change** – a reaction where new products are created which can't be turned back into what they were before the reaction.

**Liquid** – a state of matter in which the particles are loosely held together. Liquids can be poured and change their shape to fit the container they're in.

**Mass** – a measure of the amount of matter in an object.

**Matter** – anything that takes up space and has mass. The three states of matter are solid, liquid and gas.

**Mechanical energy** – the energy that an object has when it is moving.

**Melting** – the process of heating up a solid into a liquid.

# GLOSSARY

**Melting point** – the temperature at which a solid melts into a liquid.

**Method** – the process of carrying out the experiment or test and getting results.

**Microscopic** – invisible to the human eye without the use of a microscope (a scientific instrument that can be used to observe very small objects, such as cells).

**Microscopic cells** – cells that are too small to be seen with the naked eye. They must be magnified (made bigger) under a microscope to become visible.

**Mixture** – two substances that are mixed together but not chemically joined.

**Molecule** – two or more atoms bonded together.

**Negative charge** – the state of having more electrons than protons.

**Neutralization** – the process of an acid reacting with an alkali to produce a solution of salt and water with a neutral pH of 7.

# GLOSSARY

**Non-Newtonian fluid** – a fluid that exhibits both liquid and solid properties. The viscosity of the fluid changes according to the amount of pressure applied.

**Opaque** – when it's not possible to see through a substance.

**Oxidation** – the process of a substance reacting with oxygen.

**Particle** – a microscopic piece of matter.

**pH** – a measurement of how acidic or alkaline a substance is.

**pH indicator** – a substance that tells you the pH of another substance by colouring it.

**pH scale** – a scale which measures how acidic or alkaline different substances are.

**Pigment** – a substance that produces a characteristic colour.

**Positive charge** – the state of having fewer electrons than protons.

**Precision** – a measurement of how close a result is to the repeated results.

# GLOSSARY

**Propane** – a heavy, flammable hydrocarbon gas made from petroleum and natural gas. It's used for home and water heating.

**Protein** – large, complex molecules that are found in certain foods, such as milk, meat and eggs.

**Reactivity** – how likely a substance is to undergo a chemical reaction, either by itself or with another substance.

**Residue** – a substance left behind after a mixture is filtered.

**Reversible change/physical change** – a change in which no new products are made and the substance can go back to what it was before the change.

**Rubidium** – a soft, silvery and highly reactive alkali metal.

**Sieving** – the process of separating solids of different sizes.

**Similar** – looking or being almost, but not exactly, the same.

**Sodium acetate** – a type of sodium salt. It's composed of one sodium atom, two oxygen atoms, two carbon atoms and three hydrogen atoms.

# GLOSSARY

**Sodium bicarbonate** – a type of sodium salt. It's composed of one sodium atom, one hydrogen atom, one carbon atom and three oxygen atoms.

**Sodium hydroxide** – a strongly alkaline compound composed of sodium, oxygen and hydrogen. It's used in the manufacture of soap and paper.

**Solid** – a state of matter in which the particles are in a fixed position. Solids do not change their shape or volume.

**Soluble** – a substance that can be dissolved into a solvent.

**Solute** – the part of a solution that is dissolved into a solvent.

**Solution** – a liquid mixture that contains a solute which is evenly spread throughout the liquid.

**Solvent** – the substance that a solute is dissolved into.

**Thermal energy** – heat energy.

**Translucent** – something that can't be seen through clearly, but which light can pass through.

**Valid** – how true the results are.

**Variable** – the component of the experiment that is changed or measured.

**Vibrating** – moving back and forth in a fixed position.

**Volume** – the amount of space that a substance takes up.

WITH THANKS TO IMAAN WALLACE FOR ALL YOUR SUPPORT
AND TO SUBI BOSA FOR HIS BRILLIANT ARTWORK